TOP **10**
SYDNEY

T000160S

Top 10 Sydney Highlights

The Top 10 of Everything

CONTENTS

Sydney
Area by Area

Streetsmart

Within each Top 10 list in this book, no hierarchy of quality or popularity is implied. All 10 are, in the editor's opinion, of roughly equal merit.

Title page, front cover and spine Sydney Opera House and Circular Quay
Back cover, clockwise from top left Sydney Harbour Bridge; The Gap, Watsons Bay; Tamarama Beach; Hyde Park

The rapid rate at which the world is changing is constantly keeping the DK Eyewitness team on our toes. While we've worked hard to ensure that this edition of Sydney is accurate and up-to-date, we know that opening hours alter, standards shift, prices fluctuate, places close and new ones pop up in their stead. So, if you notice we've got something wrong or left something out, we want to hear about it. Please get in touch at
travelguides@dk.com

Welcome to
Sydney

A glistening harbour, golden sandy beaches and glorious green spaces. Historic cobbled streets and heritage buildings hewn from local sandstone. Iconic architecture and soaring skyscrapers. Sydney effortlessly combines a relaxed outdoor lifestyle with the energy and buzz of a modern global city. With DK Eyewitness Top 10 Sydney, it's yours to explore.

Comprising a series of distinct urban villages, this multicultural capital is both cosmopolitan and historic. Nowhere is this better illustrated than **the Rocks**, where traces of the city's past lie sandwiched between the modern icons that are the **Sydney Opera House** and the **Sydney Harbour Bridge**. A vibrant mood abounds throughout the city, whether you're exploring the traditional flavours of bustling **Chinatown**, the vibrant LGBTQ+ scene of **Darlinghurst** or the glitzy boutiques of **Paddington**.

At the city's heart lies the ever-beautiful **Sydney Harbour**, forming a spectacular backdrop for countless outdoor activities. Locals spend much of their free time enjoying green harbourside oases such as **Barangaroo Reserve** and the **Royal Botanic Garden**, or relaxing on golden beaches at laid-back spots like **Bondi Beach**. Beyond the centre lie even more opportunities to connect with nature, from the soaring peaks of the **Blue Mountains** to the lush vineyards of the **Hunter Valley**.

Whether you're coming for a weekend or a week, our Top 10 guide brings together the best of everything Sydney can offer, from the bustle of the **City Centre** to the tranquillity of the **Eastern Suburbs**. The guide gives you tips throughout, from seeking out what's free to places off the beaten track, plus 10 easy-to-follow itineraries around selections of the best sights. Add inspiring photography and detailed maps, and you've got the essential pocket-sized travel companion. **Enjoy the book, and enjoy Sydney.**

Clockwise from top: Bondi Beach; Royal Botanic Garden and city skyline; Dr Chau Chak Wing Building; Sydney Opera House and Harbour Bridge at sunset; a koala; outdoor diners at Bodhi restaurant, near Hyde Park; the Three Sisters in the Blue Mountains.

Exploring Sydney

To see Sydney's top sights, stick to the sea; most of the city's attractions can be found in and around the harbour. Whether you have a couple of days in the city or are staying for longer, here are some ideas for two and four days of sightseeing in Sydney.

The Chinese Garden of Friendship is an oasis of calm at the heart of the city.

Key

— Two-day itinerary
— Four-day itinerary

Two Days in Sydney

Day ❶

MORNING

Wander the backstreets of **the Rocks** (see pp22–3) and then take the pedestrian walkway onto the **Sydney Harbour Bridge** (see p16–17). Climb the **Pylon Lookout** (see p17) before a pub lunch at the famous **Lord Nelson Brewery Hotel** (see p93).

AFTERNOON

Follow the **Writers' Walk** (see p22) along **Circular Quay** (see pp22–3) and stroll around the **Sydney Opera House** (see pp12–15). Walk through the **Royal Botanic Garden** (see pp24–7) to the **Art Gallery of New South Wales** (see pp30–31).

Day ❷

MORNING

Feel the sand between your toes at **Bondi Beach** (see pp40–41), and take the magnificent **Coastal Walk** (see p60) to the beach at Bronte before heading back to the city.

AFTERNOON

Stroll through **Chinatown** (see pp34–5) and get a legendary cream puff at **Emperor's Garden Cakes and Bakery** (see p92). Continue to **Darling Harbour** (see pp34–5) and join the locals at play. Follow **Wulugal Walk** through **Barangaroo** (see pp36–7) before experiencing **Sydney Harbour** (see pp18–19) with a ferry ride to **Circular Quay** (see pp22–3).

Four Days in Sydney

Day ❶

MORNING

Peruse the works at the **Museum of Contemporary Art** (see p23) and then meander to the **Sydney Opera House** (see pp12–13) for a one-hour tour. Break the day with lunch at Portside.

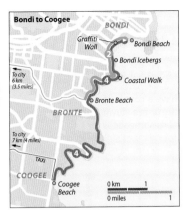

Bondi to Coogee

BONDI

Graffiti Wall

Bondi Beach

Bondi Icebergs

Coastal Walk

Bronte Beach

BRONTE

TAXI

COOGEE

Coogee Beach

To city 6 km (3.5 miles)

To city 7 km (4 miles)

FERRY

To Taronga Zoo 2 km (1.2 miles)

Portside

Sydney Opera House

Writers' Walk

Royal Botanic Garden

Art Gallery of New South Wales

Sydney Harbour

e Park

TAXI

From Bronte beach 6 km (3.5 miles)

Coogee beach 7 km (4 miles)

0 km   1
0 miles   1

AFTERNOON
Take a ferry to Pyrmont (see pp120–25) and visit Darling Harbour's illuminating **Australian National Maritime Museum** (see p48). Cross over **Pyrmont Bridge** (see p35) and wander onto Dixon Street for a spot of souvenir shopping in **Chinatown** (see pp34–5).

Day ❷
MORNING
Explore **the Rocks'** (see pp22–3) cobbled streets and learn about the area's fascinating history at the Rocks Discovery Museum. After, walk along the **Sydney Harbour Bridge** (see pp16–17) pedestrian deck and visit the lofty **Pylon Lookout** (see p17) for stunning city views.
AFTERNOON
Take a scenic ferry to **Taronga Zoo** (see pp38–9) from **Circular Quay** (see pp22–3) and visit the native animals in the Australian Walkabout exhibit.

Day ❸
MORNING
Explore the works in the **Art Gallery of New South Wales** (see pp30–31), followed by a picnic lunch in the **Royal Botanic Garden** (see pp24–7).
AFTERNOON
Admire the historic buildings along **Macquarie Street** (see p28) on your way to **Hyde Park** (see p88). Gaze towards the Blue Mountains from **Sydney Tower** (see p89) before continuing to **Queen Victoria Building** (see p88). Round off with a drink at **Barangaroo** (see pp36–7).

Day ❹
MORNING
Hit the sand at **Bondi Beach** (see pp40–41) and then have lunch at **Icebergs Dining Room** (see p111).
AFTERNOON
Take the exhilarating clifftop **Coastal Walk** (see p41) to Coogee. Later on head to the **Sydney Opera House** (see pp12–15) for dinner and the stunning **Badu Gili** (see p12) light projection.

Beautiful Tamarama Beach forms part of the Bondi to Coogee coastal walk.

Top 10 Sydney Highlights

**The distinctive sails of
Sydney Opera House**

🔟 Sydney Highlights

Sydney is blessed with stunning ocean beaches, magnificent national parks and a subtropical climate that makes the great outdoors irresistible to its five million inhabitants. It is at once a lively, vibrant metropolis, with a buzzing arts and social scene, and a laid-back city, where days can be spent chilling harbourside. Here are some of the city's top attractions.

Sydney Opera House ①
Sydney's architectural icon and performing arts venue enjoys the most spectacular setting of any cultural institution in the world *(see pp12–15)*.

② Sydney Harbour Bridge
This enormous and beautiful structure, an economic and engineering triumph, reshaped Sydney's landscape forever *(see pp16–17)*.

③ Sydney Harbour
From its pristine beaches to its working docklands, this deepwater port is supremely picturesque *(see pp18–21)*.

④ The Rocks and Circular Quay
The First Fleet's arrival here in 1788 began Australia's European settlement. Now it's an engaging historic precinct *(see pp22–3)*.

⑤ Royal Botanic Garden and the Domain
Lying east of the city centre, the Domain incorporates the Royal Botanic Garden and has been one of Sydney's best-loved green spaces for over 200 years *(see pp24–9)*.

6 Art Gallery of New South Wales
Featuring one of the country's most impressive and extensive collections of Australian and international art, this striking gallery is not to be missed *(see pp30–33)*.

7 Darling Harbour and Chinatown
The hustle and bustle of Chinatown's eateries and markets gives way to the waterfront playground that is Darling Harbour, with its many bars and tourist attractions *(see pp34–5)*.

8 Barangaroo
This vibrant waterfront precinct on the western harbour foreshore includes an expansive nature reserve and many bars and restaurants *(see pp36–7)*.

Map labels: Mosman Bay; RAGLAN ST; PRINCE ALBERT ST; BRADLEYS HEAD RD; Taronga Zoo 9; CREMORNE POINT; Whiting Beach; Athol Bay; rraba int; Robertsons Point; S y d n e y   H a r b o u r; Bradleys Head; Fort Denison 3; acquaries; 0 metres 800; 0 yards 800; Clark Island; POTTS POINT; Elizabeth Bay; DARLING POINT; KINGS CROSS; Rushcutters Bay; RUSHCUTTERS BAY; MONA RD; BAYSWATER RD; UNDARY ST; NEILD AVE; GLENMORE ROAD; CASCADE ST; HARGRAVE RD; Trumper Park; PADDINGTON; 5 km (3 miles) 10

9 Taronga Zoo
The zoo's collection of Australian and non-native animals, not to mention its gorgeous setting overlooking the harbour, makes it a perennially popular destination for visitors *(see pp38–9)*.

10 Bondi Beach
Sydney's swimmers and surfers all love Australia's most iconic beach. Don't leave the city without spending some special moments here *(see pp40–41)*.

TOP 10 ⭐ Sydney Opera House

The Opera House's magnificent harbourside location, stunning architecture and excellent programme of events make it Sydney's number one destination. This modern masterpiece reflects the genius of its architect, Jørn Utzon – his design triumphed over 232 others submitted for the Opera House international design competition. The site now welcomes 11 million visitors every year.

1 Forecourt and Monumental Steps

Framed by the Royal Botanic Garden and Government House, the Forecourt and the wide Monumental Steps **(above)** are the perfect setting for outdoor events and form the Opera House's largest performance space. Events held here include concerts by international artists.

2 Concert Hall

This is the biggest room in the Opera House, seating 2,679 people. Features include a high vaulted ceiling and the Grand Organ, which has 10,244 pipes and took over 10 years to build.

3 Drama Theatre

This intimate theatre was not part of Utzon's original plan. Today, however, it is a much-loved venue for plays **(below)** with good sightlines from every part of the room.

Sydney Opera House

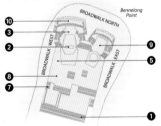

4 Badu Gili

This free six-minute projection on the eastern Bennelong sail of the Opera House explores First Nations stories in spectacular style. The name means "water light" and the best views are to be had from the Monumental Steps.

5 The Studio

The Studio is a versatile space where big creative ideas are showcased. Seating 300 people, it hosts experimental music performances, cabaret, comedy shows, circus acts and much more.

7 Backstage Tour

Take a peek behind the curtains with a guided, two-hour early morning tour, finishing with breakfast in the Green Room where artists prepare for shows. Prior booking is essential.

BENNELONG

Sydney Opera House stands on Bennelong Point, named for the first Aboriginal man to visit Europe and return. In 1789, at the age of 25, Bennelong was abducted from Manly Cove to work as Governor Arthur Phillip's translator; he escaped several months later, but subsequently returned to the role voluntarily. In 1792 he travelled with Phillip to London, where he was presented to King George III. After returning to Sydney in 1795, he chose to spend the rest of his life within his own Aboriginal community.

9 Joan Sutherland Theatre

Named for Australia's greatest operatic soprano, this lovely theatre is home to the Australian Ballet, the Sydney Dance Company and Opera Australia.

6 Roof

Comprising ten "sails", the roof **(above)** is made of over one million ceramic tiles. These take on a luminous glow at dawn and dusk.

8 Playhouse

This intimate venue hosts music, dance, theatre productions and the "Kids and Families" arts programme.

NEED TO KNOW

MAP N1 ■ Bennelong Point ■ www.sydneyopera house.com

Open for performances and tours (10:30am, noon and 2pm daily; adm)

Badu Gili: four screenings from sunset daily

Backstage Tour: 7am daily; adm

■ There's a variety of places to eat and drink at the Opera House. Book an outdoor table at Portside, enjoy fine dining at Bennelong *(see p93)*, cocktails at Opera Bar *(see p74)* or choose from an array of options at the Opera Kitchen, a food hall that has a bakery and a pasta bar.

10 Northern Foyers

Topaz-tinted glass canopies and massive girders **(above)** enclose the Northern Foyers of the Concert Hall and Joan Sutherland Theatre, with spectacular views of the harbour.

Construction Timeline

1 1954
Eugene Goosens, the Conservatorium of Music's director, lobbied the state Labor Premier, Joseph Cahill, to construct an opera house. Cahill appointed Goosens to a committee investigating the proposal.

2 1956
Upon Goosens' return from an overseas conducting tour, customs agents mysteriously found what was then considered "pornography" in his luggage. He resigned immediately and returned to Europe leaving an overwrought media frenzy in his wake.

3 1957
The Danish architect Jørn Utzon was declared the winner of an international competition to design the new opera house. The project was projected to cost $7 million and be completed in 1963.

4 1958
Demolition of the old tram sheds along Bennelong Point commenced. Following an unsuccessful fundraising venture, the government established the Opera House Lottery to cover the estimated costs of construction.

5 1959
Premier Cahill responded to public and media concern about project delays and rising costs.

He insisted that work commence. Utzon and the project engineer Ove Arup protested, asserting their plans were incomplete. Work started on the platform (Stage 1).

6 1960–62
Utzon was able to resolve the dilemma of the roof's design and construction in 1961. Eugene Goosens died in 1962.

7 1963–65
Work started on the roof (Stage 2). In 1965 a Liberal/Country Party Coalition elected to office promised to stem costs and delays.

People's protest march, 1966

8 1966
On 28 February, Utzon resigned after disputes with the government over designs, deadlines and fees. The public protested vigorously.

9 1966–73
The Northern Foyers, interiors, walkways and concourse were completed (Stage 3).

10 1973
A large crowd gathered at the Forecourt on 20 October 1973 to watch Queen Elizabeth II formally declare the Sydney Opera House open. Final cost: $102 million.

Discussing the Opera House design plans, February 1959

DESIGNING THE SYDNEY OPERA HOUSE

Jørn Utzon

Inspired by the fan-like ribs of a palm leaf, Utzon's intention was to construct a timeless structure that blended in with its natural surroundings. The roof "shells" were to float above the harbour like giant sails. Utzon's early drawings were inspired, but didn't allow for cost-effective prefabrication. In partnership with the London-based engineering firm Ove Arup & Partners, Utzon laboured for months over the issue. His elegant epiphany came in 1961. If the shells were all cast from the same sphere, thus sharing a radius, it would be possible to pre-cast the concrete ribs as segments which could later be assembled. Work began on the roof in 1963 and, despite numerous delays, disagreements and wrangling over designs and fees, was completed ten years later. In 2003 Utzon's genius was recognized by the architecture world's equivalent of the Nobel Prize, the Pritzker Prize. Following Utzon's death in 2008, a state memorial was held in the concert hall.

TOP 10 MEMORABLE MOMENTS

1 1960: Singer Paul Robeson performs for construction workers.

2 1973: A possum appears at the house's first production.

3 1975: Maxim Shostakovich conducts his father Dmitri's Symphony Number 10.

4 1983: Joan Sutherland and Luciano Pavarotti perform the "Concert of the Century".

5 1986: Pope John Paul II addresses religious orders in the concert hall.

6 1990: Nelson Mandela gives a public address.

7 1990: Joan Sutherland gives her last performance.

8 1992: Peter Allen performs for the last time.

9 2003: Protesters daub "No War" on the roof in protest at Australia's involvement in Iraq.

10 2006: Elizabeth II opens the Colonnade.

Construction of the shell-shaped roof, well underway in June 1966.

TOP 10 ⭐ Sydney Harbour Bridge

Affectionately known as the "coathanger" to Sydneysiders, this is the world's largest and widest steel arch bridge. Construction began in 1923 and took eight years, 53,000 tonnes of steel and six million hand-driven rivets to complete. The bridge links the southern and northern sides of the harbour with eight lanes of traffic, two railway lines and pedestrian and cycle paths. It is the focal point of Sydney's New Year's Eve fireworks display, and its sweeping lines have captivated artists since its opening in 1932.

1 Design
Built by Dorman Long & Co from engineer John Bradfield's design, the bridge features decorative granite-clad pylons by Sir John Burnet & Partners.

2 Bradfield Park
Under the northern pylons **(left)**, this small park commemorating John Bradfield offers unparalleled views of the Opera House and Circular Quay. Directly beneath the bridge is the bow of the original HMAS *Sydney*.

3 A Second Crossing
The Sydney Harbour Tunnel – a twin-tube road tunnel running under the harbour – was opened in 1992 to reduce traffic congestion on the bridge as the city grew and became busier.

5 Maintenance
It takes 30,000 litres (6,599 gal) of paint annually to keep the structure sound. Actor Paul Hogan worked as a painter on the bridge before he made it big as Crocodile Dundee.

6 Dawes Point
Below the southern pylons is the site of the Sydney colony's first observatory, built in 1788. The park's interpretation boards and the excavated remains of the fort that replaced the observatory offer an interesting perspective on the city's development.

4 BridgeClimb
Since BridgeClimb **(below)** opened for business in 1998, more than four million people have climbed the bridge. The 3.5-hour guided climb over the top of the arch is exhilarating and there is no better way to appreciate the enormity and beauty of the structure.

AN UNOFFICIAL OPENING

Before Premier Jack Lang could cut the ceremonial ribbon at the bridge's opening in 1932, a man swept forward and slashed it with a sword. "Captain" Francis de Groot declared the bridge open in the name of "decent citizens of New South Wales". He belonged to the right-wing New Guard, which opposed Lang's "socialist" government and believed that only royalty should inaugurate the bridge.

7 Pedestrian and Cycle Paths

The free stroll across the eastern-side pedestrian walkway (**left**) is an excellent way to experience the bridge. There is also a free cycle path on the western side.

8 Famous Portraits

Works by renowned artists such as Grace Cossington-Smith, Dorrit Black, Gwen Barringer and Henri Mallard reflect the optimism inspired by the bridge in the midst of the Great Depression. Their pictures hang in the city's art galleries and museums and honour the bravery of those who worked on the bridge.

9 Pylon Lookout and Museum

A long climb up 200 stairs to the top of the southeast pylon, 87 m (285 ft) above the harbour, reveals fabulous 360-degree views. Three levels of exhibits explore the history of the bridge along the way. Access to the pylon is via the pedestrian path.

10 Memorial

During the Great Depression in the 1930s more than 2,000 people worked on the bridge, many riding crane hooks without safety harnesses. A plaque on the southern approach to the bridge commemorates the 16 workers who lost their lives during the construction process.

The DNEY MAIL
SOUVENIR BRIDGE NUMBER
PRICE 6D

The commemorative issue of the *Sydney Mail*

NEED TO KNOW

MAP D2

BridgeClimb:
3 Cumberland St, The Rocks; open daily, check website for times; adm (prices rise at twilight, at weekends and in peak season: 25 Dec–5 Jan); www.bridgeclimb.com

Pedestrian path entry:
Cumberland St, The Rocks

Cycle path entry:
Observatory Park

Pylon Lookout:
Cumberland St; 10am–5pm daily; closed 25 Dec; adm (under 5s free); www.pylonlookout.com.au

■ Enjoy a cocktail on the rooftop of the Harbour View Hotel (www.harbourview.com.au).

■ For a unique view of the bridge from the northern side, ride the Ferris wheel at Luna Park (www.lunaparksydney.com).

TOP 10 ⭐ Sydney Harbour

It took the Parramatta and Lane Cove rivers thousands of years to carve Sydney Harbour – arguably the most beautiful in the world – from sandstone. Aboriginal peoples lived along the harbour foreshore as far west as Parramatta before the British arrived and established their first colony here in 1788. From its working docklands to its pristine and secluded beaches, this harbour is a natural asset that most cities can only dream of.

Harbourside Walks ①

Sydney offers a wide range of great harbourside walks **(right)**, thanks to the Harbour Foreshore Vigilance Committee (see p101), formed in 1905 to retain harbourside land for public use.

HMAS KUTTABUL

Three Japanese midget submarines passed through Sydney Heads on 31 May 1942. One sub aimed at the US naval ship *Chicago* but its torpedo missed and sank a dormitory ship for Australian and British soldiers, the HMAS *Kuttabul*. The *Kuttabul* sank within minutes and 21 soldiers died. A chase ensued: one vessel escaped, while the other two sank. These two subs were later recovered and their Japanese crew members were cremated with full naval honours in recognition by Australia of their bravery.

② The Working Harbour

View the harbour's working history at the Australian National Maritime Museum (see p34), wander Balmain's backstreets or discover the convict and maritime history of Cockatoo Island (see p122).

③ Harbourside Parks

While some parks offer extensive walking trails, others are lush pockets of shaded greenery. The best parks include Balls Head Reserve (see p127), the Royal Botanic Garden (see pp24–27) and Barangaroo (see pp36–7).

④ Sydney Harbour National Park

This remarkable national park includes seven islands. Aboriginal rock art sites, historic buildings, secluded beaches, monuments, lookouts and bushwalks are just some of its highlights. The National Parks and Wildlife Service (NPWS) manages the park and operates several tours.

NEED TO KNOW

MAP F2

Sydney Harbour National Park: 1300 072 757; www.nationalparks.nsw.gov.au

■ Pack a picnic and head to Shark Island. Captain Cook Cruises (see pp142–3) operates ferry services to Shark Island at weekends and on some weekdays during school holidays. National Park landing fees are included in the price.

⑤ Harbour Beaches

Sydney's harbour beaches are glorious, including Shark Beach **(above)** and Manly Cove (see p130). Parsley Bay, Camp Cove and Lady Bay Beach in Watsons Bay are all gems and are accessible by ferry. Several beaches have protective shark netting.

⑥ Harbour Wildlife

Sydney Harbour is a remarkably healthy wildlife habitat, home to rainbow lorikeets, several species of shark and fish, sea horses, dolphins, the occasional whale and the only known Little Penguin **(right)** breeding colony on the Australian mainland.

⑨ The Heads

The rugged South and North Heads (see p58–9) offer magnificent ocean and harbour views. They are particularly popular on Boxing Day when crowds gather to cheer the start of the Sydney to Hobart yacht race (see p83).

⑦ Naval Bases

Sydney harbour has served as a naval base for the Royal Australian Navy ever since the early days of European settlement, with the dockyard at Garden Island in Woolloomooloo the traditional centre of naval activity.

⑧ Harbourside Residences

Among the fancy homes here are Boomerang (see p97), built for music publisher Frank Albert, Craigend (Darling Point, originally owned by magnate James Patrick), and Russell Crowe's penthouse at Finger Wharf in Woolloomooloo.

⑩ Ferry Rides

No trip to Sydney is complete without a ferry ride (see pp20–21). A journey to Manly is the classic trip, but other popular destinations include Watsons Bay, Balmain, Mosman and Darling Harbour.

Sydney Harbour

On the Water

Ferry plying a route across the harbour

1 Ferries
www.transportnsw.info
The most inexpensive way to experience the harbour is by taking one of the 32 public ferries that service almost 40 destinations.

2 Harbour and Rivercats
If you plan to visit Sydney Olympic Park or Parramatta's historic attractions, avoid the congestion of Parramatta Road by taking one of the sleek River Class Ferries. If you're in a rush to reach Manly Beach, hop on the Fast Ferry for the 20-minute trip.

3 Spectator Ferry
18 Footers League:
www.18footers.com
Catch a spectator ferry and follow the fast-moving and elegant skiffs as they race on weekends from September to March.

4 Water Taxis
Although too expensive for daily commuting, these taxis are a fun option if you fancy a peek at the luxurious harbourside mansions or a picnic on one of the islands.

5 Catamarans
Several gigantic catamarans service the harbour tourist trade. In some cases you can enjoy an onboard BBQ, or work on your tan as you cruise the harbour.

6 Jet Boats
Operators: www.sydney jet.com; www.ozjetboating.com
If you feel the "need for speed" on the water, Sydney Harbour's jet boats will definitely give you an adrenaline fix to remember.

7 Tall Ships
www.sydneytallships.com.au
Embark on a discovery, lunch or twilight dinner cruise in a traditional square-rigged vessel with Sydney Harbour Tall Ships.

8 Boats for Rent
Rent anything from sea canoes to 4-m (14-ft) aluminium boats to 6-m (20-ft) half-cabin cruisers. On a kayak you can explore Middle Harbour at your own leisurely pace.

Sydney Harbour seaplane

9 Sea-planes
Flights around Sydney Harbour offer excellent fly-and-dine packages and can also take you to the gorgeous Northern Beaches, Pittwater and Hawkesbury regions.

10 Helicopters
For a bird's-eye view of the harbour, board a helicopter for an exciting and scenic ride over the Harbour Bridge, the Opera House, Eastern Suburbs and Manly Cove.

SAILING ON SYDNEY HARBOUR

Sailing in the harbour

Sydney Harbour is perfect for sailing, although sometimes you can't see the water for the canvas. Wednesday afternoons and weekends are popular with the more competitive old salts, especially in the racing season, which runs between September and March. Friday twilight sailing is perfect for the more laid-back yachtie. Several firms, including Sydney Harbour Escapes, rent yachts for bareboat charter and offer social sailing and sailing lessons. Balmain Sailing Club's Sailing School, Sydney by Sail and East Sail can also show you the ropes. *Afloat* is a free monthly magazine for the yachting fraternity and for those with an interest in Sydney's maritime history. It also carries a regular calendar of events, tide charts and fishing tips. Check the Crew Wanted classifieds if you fancy running away to sea. *Afloat* is available at all marinas and online *(www.afloat.com.au)*.

On busy weekends during the summer, Sydney Harbour is awash with sails.

TOP 10 FAMOUS HARBOURSIDE RESIDENTS

1 Chris Hemsworth, actor

2 Nicole Kidman, actor

3 Judy Davis & Colin Friels, actors

4 Malcolm Turnbull, former prime minister

5 Mike Cannon-Brookes, tech billionaire

6 Russell Crowe, actor

7 May Gibbs, author

8 Hugo Weaving, actor

9 Cate Blanchett, actor

10 Rebel Wilson, actor

Cate Blanchett

TOP 10 ⭐ The Rocks and Circular Quay

Near the maritime centre of Circular Quay, the Rocks is a mainly residential precinct of narrow laneways, galleries, boutiques and restaurants. Originally known as Tallawoladah by the Gadigal people, the peninsula that houses the Rocks is where the First Fleet arrived on 26 January 1788. Within days, they had established a settlement beneath the sandstone outcrops that gave the Rocks its name.

1 Circular Quay

This maritime hub **(right)** is Sydney's nucleus. Plaques in the paving along Sydney Writer's Walk record observations by authors such as Umberto Eco, Mark Twain and Germaine Greer.

2 Rocks Discovery Museum

A free, small museum housed in a restored 1850s sandstone ware-house, this collection shines a fascinating light on both the First Nations and colonial history of the area.

5 Susannah Place Museum

Built in 1844, this heritage-listed former grocery store and row of workers' cottages now serves as a historic museum **(below)** in Sydney's oldest quarter.

3 George Street

Australia's oldest street runs through the heart of the Rocks and is now a busy stretch of boutiques, galleries, shops and pubs. The Rocks Market **(above)**, selling crafts, jewellery and the like, is held at the northern end of the street at weekends.

4 Garrison Church

Australia's first military church is officially named Holy Trinity Church. Designed by Henry Ginn in 1840, it was remodelled in 1878 by Edmund Blacket, architect of the main building at the University of Sydney (see p115).

6 Customs House

Renovations of this stately 1844 building **(left)** have seen the addition of a major public library. Customs House also hosts a wide range of exhibitions and events.

7 Cadman's Cottage and Sailors' Home

Built in 1816, this is Sydney's oldest surviving dwelling. The sandstone cottage accommodated the government coxswain, and later, the water transport headquarters. The building was originally situated on the waterfront.

8 Overseas Passenger Terminal

A stylish glass structure containing excellent bars and restaurants; its 1988 renovation replaced the 1950s terminal that once accommodated passenger liners.

LIEUTENANT WILLIAM DAWES

Lieutenant Dawes established Australia's first observatory on the point that now bears his name. In 1790 he earned Governor Phillip's displeasure when he refused to join a reprisal attack against First Nations peoples. His refusal sprang from his relationship with a Gadigal woman, Patyegarang. Dawes' journals detail his conversations with Patyegarang and discuss the vocabulary and grammar of the Gadigal.

The Rocks and Circular Quay

---

9 Museum of Contemporary Art (MCA)

The cutting-edge MCA displays contemporary art from Australia and around the world. It offers tours, exhibitions and lectures, and is also home to the innovative National Centre for Creative Learning.

10 Sydney Observatory

This 1858 Italianate building **(below)** was converted into a museum of astronomy in 1988. The tower's time-ball still drops daily at 1pm, while a cannon is fired simultaneously from Fort Denison in the harbour (see pp18–19).

TOP 10 ⭐ Royal Botanic Garden and the Domain

This tranquil part of Sydney was once used by the Gadigal people for fishing and camping, before becoming the home of the Royal Botanic Garden in 1816. A green oasis in the heart of the city, it is the perfect place for a stroll. Macquarie Street marks the western boundary of this area, named for an early governor and built as a ceremonial thoroughfare of civic buildings.

MRS BIGGS' BATHING BOX

The colony's first public baths, the Fig Tree Baths, stood on the site of the Andrew "Boy" Charlton Pool overlooking Woolloomooloo Bay, a home of the Gadigal people. Several businesses once catered to the delicate sensibilities of Sydney's bathers, including one owned by a Mrs Biggs. An artwork by Robyn Backen, *The Archaeology of Bathing*, recalls Mrs Biggs' 1833 Bathing Machine, designed to protect the modesty of her patrons from bothersome gazes as well as sharks.

The Domain ③

Sydneysiders gather for free outdoor community events at this large open space **(right)** on Art Gallery Road. These include jazz and opera performances, music festivals and Carols in the Domain, at 8pm on the last Saturday before Christmas.

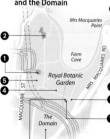

④ Walks and Tours

The Royal Botanic Garden's volunteers conduct guided walks. A heritage tour explores First Nations culture and its connection to the land, including how plants were used in Aboriginal medicine.

Royal Botanic Garden and the Domain

① Conservatorium of Music

Designed by Francis Greenway *(see p29)*, this grandiose building was originally the stables for the first Government House. "The Con" has been training Sydney's musical talent since 1915.

② Government House

George Gipps was the first governor to occupy this Gothic Revival structure **(below)** in 1845. The house and grounds retain much of their original character.

⑤ Palace Rose Garden

A colourful, fragrant garden with themed displays of roses in "formal", "flamboyant" and "romantic" beds.

⑥ Cadi Jam Ora: First Encounters Garden

This award-winning presentation of the Gadigal people's story offers a fascinating look at the impact of white settlement, Sydney's environment and the Gadigal's spiritual connection with their land.

⑧ Andrew "Boy" Charlton Pool

Named for a 16-year-old Olympic winner, this glorious 50-m (164-ft) heated saltwater swimming pool **(right)** overlooks Woolloomooloo Bay and Garden Island. Glass fencing surrounds the pool and maximizes the location's beauty.

⑦ Palm House

The Victorian-era glasshouse was designed by James Barnet to display tropical plants. The Palm House is now used for art exhibitions and the plants are in the Sydney Tropical Centre.

⑨ Wollemi Pine

Rediscovered in 1994 in a Blue Mountains canyon *(see p133)*, this ancient botanical curiosity was thought to be long extinct. The specimen that stands in the Royal Botanic Garden was planted in 1998.

⑩ Mrs Macquarie's Chair

This sandstone bench **(left)** was hand-carved in 1816 for the governor's wife, Elizabeth Macquarie. The landmark offers breathtaking views of the Opera House, Harbour Bridge and Fort Denison.

NEED TO KNOW

MAP N3 ▣ Royal Botanic Garden ▣ Mrs Macquaries Rd ▣ www.rbgsyd.nsw.gov.au

Open 7am–sunset daily

Walks and Tours: 9231 8317; tours depart from the garden shop daily, check website for times

Conservatorium of Music: www.sydney.edu.au

Andrew "Boy" Charlton Pool: Mrs Macquaries Rd; open Sep–Apr: 6am–8pm daily; closed for special events, check website for details; adm; www.abcpool.org

Government House: House tours 10:30am–3pm at 30-minute intervals Fri–Sun; gardens open 10am–4pm Fri–Sun; ID required; www.governor.nsw.org.au

▣ Farm Cove Eatery is a casual dining spot in the Royal Botanic Garden where you can either eat in or get a picnic to take away and enjoy in the gardens (www.botanichouse.com.au).

Following pages *A shaded alley in the Royal Botanic Garden*

Macquarie Street Precinct

1 The Astor
One of Sydney's first skyscrapers, this elegant 13-storey 1920s apartment building has housed famous creatives such as actor Cate Blanchett.

2 State Library of New South Wales
More than five million books, maps and other items are held in the Library's Mitchell (1910) and Macquarie (1988) wings *(see p88)*. The exhibition spaces showcase this vast collection and also host talks.

3 Parliament House
The oldest parliament house in Australia began in 1816 as a wing of the "Rum Hospital", built in lieu of payment of duty by contractors licensed to import rum.

4 Martin Place
Australia's grandest banks reside on this broad plaza *(see p90)*. A nearby cenotaph commemorates Australia's war dead, and a bronze sculpture entitled *Passage* by local artist Anne Graham celebrates Sydney's Georgian heritage.

5 Sydney Hospital
This structure replaced the central wing of the Rum Hospital in the 1880s. The statue of a boar outside the building, *Il Porcellino*, is a replica of a 1547 Florentine artwork by Pietro Tacca.

The boar statue at Sydney Hospital

6 The Mint
This elegant building is home to the Sydney Living Museums' head office. Formerly an 1816 Rum Hospital wing, it now houses offices, venue hire spaces, a public library, restaurant and café.

Interior of St James Church

7 St James Church
Built by Francis Greenway, this 1822 church was originally intended as a courthouse. Don't miss the superb 1930s mural in the Children's Chapel.

8 Hyde Park Barracks Museum
Perhaps Francis Greenway's finest work, this barracks was built in 1819 to house convicts. Since 1979 it has been a museum of the site *(see p48)*.

9 Great Irish Famine Memorial
This memorial commemorates the victims of the Famine (1845–48), a catastrophe that resulted in 30,000 Irish women and over 4,000 orphans being resettled in Australia to meet a demand for domestic servants.

10 Queen's Square
Governor Macquarie viewed this small square as Sydney's civic centre. In the 1890s it was a rallying point for protesters, who would mount Queen Victoria's statue to address the crowds.

FRANCIS GREENWAY: GOVERNMENT ARCHITECT

Hyde Park Barracks

Much of historic Sydney was influenced by the work of Francis Howard Greenway. In 1809, when he was a partner in an English architectural firm, Greenway was found guilty of forging a contract and was sentenced to 14 years in the colony. Soon after his arrival in 1814, Governor Macquarie realized that Greenway's architectural talent was equal to his own Enlightenment aspirations, and in 1816 he appointed Greenway as Colonial Architect and Assistant Engineer. Starting with the Macquarie Lighthouse on South Head, Greenway and Governor and Mrs Macquarie set about transforming Sydney's civic landscape. Unfortunately, not everyone shared their ambitions, and reports of extravagance filtered back to London. Commissioner J T Bigge arrived in Sydney in 1819 to investigate and halted most public works. His censure of the Macquaries' taste for ornamentation deprived Greenway of his patrons, who departed the colony in 1822. Despite his major contribution to the standard of colonial architecture, Greenway struggled in private practice and died a poor man in 1837.

TOP 10
GREENWAY DESIGNS

1 Hyde Park Barracks, originally built to house convicts (see p48)

2 St James Church, the oldest church building in Sydney (see p28)

3 Macquarie Lighthouse, the first lighthouse in Australia (see p108)

4 St Mathew's Anglican Church and Rectory in Windsor (see p136)

5 Conservatorium of Music, still home to one of Australia's leading music schools (see p24)

6 Cleveland House, built for influential merchant Daniel Cooper

7 Old Government House, timber portico

8 Obelisk of Distances in Macquarie Place, the "zero point" for measuring road distances in NSW

9 Fort Macquarie, once stood on the site of Sydney Opera House

10 St Luke's Anglican Church in the suburb of Liverpool

A long line of replica convict hammocks extends across the third floor of the Hyde Park Barracks.

🔟 ⭐ Art Gallery of New South Wales

Conceived in the 1870s and opened to the public in 1909, the Art Gallery of New South Wales (AGNSW) contains some of the finest artworks in Australia. More than a million visitors each year enjoy its permanent collections of world art. The gallery is set to double in size with the addition of a standalone building, scheduled to open in late 2022. This is connected to the original building by a public art garden and will incorporate three art pavilions.

1 Australian Art Galleries

Featuring major names in Australian art, these galleries display works by luminaries such as Sidney Nolan, Grace Cossington-Smith, Thomas William Roberts, Roy de Maistre, Margaret Preston and Russell Drysdale. There are many paintings and sculptures by Sydney artists, both past and present *(see p32)*.

2 Original Exterior

Walter Liberty Vernon designed the striking colonnaded entrance and ornamented walls of this structure in the Classical style **(right)**.

3 Art Garden

Providing a shaded link between the gallery's old and new buildings, the Art Garden features sculptural works and creative landscaping.

4 Asian Galleries

One of the largest pan-Asian displays of art in the southern hemisphere, including intricate calligraphy, traditional and modern paintings, textiles, porcelain and Buddhist art. The space also includes a functioning Japanese tearoom.

NEED TO KNOW

MAP N3 ▪ Art Gallery Rd, The Domain ▪ 9225 1744 ▪ www.artgallery. nsw.gov.au

Open 10am–5pm daily (to 9pm Wed).

▪ Café at the Gallery (in the original building) is open 10am–3pm daily.

▪ Visit the Study Room to see works on paper that are not on display (it's best to book in advance: 9225 1758).

▪ Experience the world of Brett Whiteley *(see p32)*, by visiting the Art Gallery of New South Wales Brett Whiteley Studio in Surry Hills *(see p102)*.

5 Contemporary Galleries

An entire floor of galleries dedicated to contemporary art. They feature a vibrant selection of international and Australian works by artists such as Anish Kapoor and Fiona Hall.

6 Oil Tank Gallery

This underground art space was repurposed from a decommissioned World War II naval oil tank that supplied nearby Garden Island naval yard. It is designed to present large-scale contemporary works, installations and site-specific performances.

7 Archibald, Wynne and Sulman Prizes

At an annual in-house exhibition, several prestigious art prizes are awarded. The Archibald Prize is for portraits, the Sulman for genre painting and the Wynne for landscape painting.

8 Art After Hours

On Wednesday nights, the gallery draws a keen evening crowd with a diverse programme of events such as free film screenings, celebrity talks and live music, as well as access to the usual exhibitions.

9 Grand Courts

These rooms contain the first works acquired by the AGNSW; they largely feature British art **(above)**, which was initially the gallery's main focus. The lovely rooms complement the many noteworthy works.

10 Aboriginal and Torres Strait Islander Gallery

Dedicated to Australian First Nations art and culture, the exhibits in this internationally renowned collection range from bark paintings to works by contemporary Aboriginal artists.

A GALLERY ON THE MOVE

AGNSW's first collection was displayed at Clarke's Assembly Hall located in Elizabeth Street in April 1875. In 1880 the collection moved to a nine-room wooden fine art annexe built in the Domain. Known as the Garden Palace, the structure and all its contents were destroyed by an unexplained fire in 1882. Government Architect Walter Vernon constructed the famous main building and façade named for him between 1886 and 1909.

The gallery's new modern expansion

Top 10 Sydney Artists

1 Brett Whiteley (1939–92)
The bad boy of Australian art, Whiteley *(see p102)* was a prodigious talent who won the trifecta of the Archibald, Wynne and Sulman prizes twice in consecutive years. He died of a heroin overdose in 1992.

2 John Olsen (b 1928)
Considered Australia's most esteemed living painter, Olsen was awarded the Order of Australia in 2001. Olsen has travelled widely in Australia and abroad, continuously mapping his travels with paintings.

3 Fiona Hall (b 1953)
One of Australia's most successful contemporary artists, Hall is also an accomplished sculptor and photographer. She represented Australia at the Venice Biennale in 2015.

4 Max Dupain (1911–92)
Dupain recorded much of Australia's architectural history through his art. However, it is for his wonderful iconoclastic 1937 photo, *The Sunbaker*, that he is most celebrated.

5 Margaret Olley (1923–2011)
Olley always painted still lifes and interiors. She received the inaugural Mosman Art Prize in 1947. In 1948 William Dobell won the Archibald for his portrait of her.

Margaret Olley

6 Daniel Boyd (b 1982)
Boyd's work concentrates on reframing European settlement from an Aboriginal perspective. He paints with numerous small, largely monochrome dots to convey the sadness of historical events.

Lloyd Rees

7 Lloyd Rees (1895–1988)
Renowned for his landscape paintings, Rees also produced hundreds of drawings, many of which are in the collection of AGNSW. He began printmaking in his 80s, and continued to etch even while losing his sight.

8 Grace Cossington-Smith (1892–1984)
Sydney's first significant female artist, she was particularly interested in form and colour. She painted still lifes, landscapes and religious subjects.

9 William Yang (b 1943)
Yang specializes in social photography documenting Sydney's thriving gay community, bringing it boldly into the spotlight.

10 Ben Quilty (b 1973)
A controversial figure, Quilty paints dynamic contemporary scene in oils about a range of social issues including the massacres of First Nations peoples. He was an official war artist in Afghanistan.

IMAGES OF SYDNEY

Artist Ken Done

Sydney's First Nations peoples recorded history through ancient rock art, but the images were symbolic rather than figurative. The European artists who arrived in the late 18th century, by contrast, began documenting the city's ever-changing landscape in a more classical Western tradition. In the early years of British settlement, Sydney was often painted as a kind of fantasy, using the familiar green slopes of England instead of the new dry, strange land. Subsequent generations, however, rejoiced in the blue skies and sparkling harbour. The construction of the Harbour Bridge inspired a new group of artists, who photographed as well as painted it, signalling the rise of Sydney as an international city. Brett Whiteley concocted luscious images of the harbour in the 1970s, and in the 1980s Ken Done made his fortune selling clothes printed with sketches of the Opera House. Now more than ever, Sydney artists create through broader, more sophisticated lenses, with an accent both on domestic social issues and the influence of Australia's Eurocentric past.

TOP 10
IMAGES OF SYDNEY

1 Watkin Tench, *A Direct North General View of Sydney Cove*, 1794

2 Eugene von Guérard, *Sydney Heads*, 1865

3 Margaret Preston, *Circular Quay*, 1925

4 Grace Cossington-Smith, *The Curve of the Bridge*, 1928–9

5 Henri Mallard, *Untitled Photograph (Sydney Harbour Bridge workers)*, c 1930

6 Max Dupain, *Sydney from Harbour Bridge Pylon*, 1982

7 Roland Wakelin, *Down the Hills to Berry's Bay*, 1958

8 Jeffrey Smart, *Australian Cahill Expressway*, 1962

9 Brett Whiteley, *The Balcony 2*, 1975

10 David Moore, *Sydney Harbour from 16,000 ft*, 1976

Sydney Heads, **painted by** Eugene von Guérard in 1865, is an atmospheric rendering of the stunningly beautiful entry to Sydney Harbour.

TOP 10 ⭐ Darling Harbour and Chinatown

Cockle Bay and what is now Chinatown was once a working harbour district where some of Sydney's poorest lived, surrounded by shipyards, cargo wharves and quarries. For the 1988 bicentenary, a huge redevelopment project transformed this site, and the area was revitalized through the aquarium, the maritime and Powerhouse museums, and the Cockle Bay and King Street Wharf developments.

1 Cockle Bay and King Street Wharves

King Street Wharf **(above)** is a social mecca for office workers. Cockle Bay comprises a three-storey hive of cafés, bars, shops and restaurants.

THE ORIGINS OF CHINATOWN

Dixon Street is now the cultural heart of Sydney's Chinese community – but it wasn't always. The 1850s Gold Rush saw Sydney's first Chinatown established in the Rocks. By the 1870s, Chinese traders largely moved to the Haymarket area. When the market drew closer to Darling Harbour in the 1920s, Chinatown settled in Dixon Street.

2 Paddy's Market

Associated with the Haymarket area for 150 years, Paddy's Market is the place to find kitsch souvenirs, from koala oven mitts to printed T-shirts, as well as fresh flowers, fruit and vegetables. Upstairs, Market City has a large food court, shops and an Asian supermarket.

Australian National Maritime Museum 3

This museum **(right)** explores Australia's relationship with the sea. Visitors can climb aboard vessels, or view interactive exhibits dealing with immigration, maritime archaeology and history *(see p48)*.

4 Darling Quarter

A vibrant precinct with two village greens that host free activities and entertainment. There are plenty of dining options here and a permanent outdoor public art exhibition that includes Luminous, the world's largest interactive digital LED light installation.

5 Pyrmont Bridge

Opened in 1902, this 369-m (1,210-ft) bridge, with a quaint copper-roofed control cabin, is the oldest electrically operated swingspan bridge in the world. It moves open to allow vessels up to 14 m (46ft) tall to enter or depart Cockle Bay.

6 WILD LIFE Sydney Zoo and SEA LIFE Sydney Aquarium

It's an all-Australian line-up at the zoo – kangaroos, koalas and Tasmanian devils all feature. At the aquarium, discover over 700 species, including sharks, rays and dugongs.

7 Chinatown

This is the spirited epicentre of Sydney's large Chinese community, where lots of restaurants vie for attention with fabric shops, grocers and jewellers. Chinatown **(right)** is best visited for the Friday night market. Chinese New Year celebrations here (Jan/Feb) are loud and spectacular.

8 Capitol Theatre

Formerly a circus and picture palace, the Capitol opened as a theatre in 1928. In 1990 a Mediterranean-blue ceiling and twinkling stars were added to the inside of the theatre. The orchestra pit at the Capitol is the largest in the country.

9 Powerhouse Museum

This former power station, completed in 1902, was redesigned and opened in 1988 as a hands-on museum. The collection has more than 500,000 artifacts and focuses on art, science, inno-vation, technology, fashion and design.

10 Chinese Garden of Friendship

The garden was China's gift to Sydney during Australia's 1988 bicen-tenary celebrations. Interpretation boards provide insights into Chinese garden design. The teahouse is a peace-ful retreat from the city.

Darling Harbour and Chinatown

NEED TO KNOW

MAP L5

Paddy's Market: Hay & Thomas sts, Haymarket; 1300 361 589; open 10am–6pm Wed–Sun; www.paddysmarkets.com.au

Market City: Haymarket (above Paddy's Market); stores open 10am–7pm daily (to 8pm Thu); www.marketcity.com.au

Australian National Maritime Museum: 2 Murray St; open 10am–4pm daily; adm; www.sea.museum

WILD LIFE Sydney Zoo: Aquarium Pier; open 9am–5pm daily (Nov–Mar: to 8pm); adm; www.wildlifesydney.com.au

SEA LIFE Sydney Aquarium: Aquarium Pier; open 10am–6pm daily; adm; www.visitsealife.com/sydney

Powerhouse Museum: 500 Harris St, Ultimo; open 10am–5pm daily (to 9pm Thu); www.maas.museum/powerhouse-museum

Chinese Garden of Friendship: Darling Harbour; open 10am–5pm daily; www.chinesegarden.com.au

■ The Darling Quarter playground *(see p67)* is a great place for younger children to let off steam.

⭐ **Barangaroo**

This former industrial container wharf site has been transformed into a lively waterfront precinct on the western harbour foreshore, the result of Australia's largest urban renewal project. The area is named after Barangaroo, an influential Gadigal woman from the Cammeraygal clan. The site comprises the peaceful Barangaroo Reserve to the north and vibrant waterfront dining, bars and retail outlets to the south, with a hotel and casino to come.

Barangaroo Reserve ①

Sydney's newest foreshore park is on one of the city's oldest industrial sites. The 6-ha (15-acre) headland, reborn as a naturalistic rocky outcrop, offers impressive harbour views, lookouts, and walking and cycling trails **(right)**.

② Wulugal Walk

This waterfront promenade **(below)** is a shared pedestrian and cyclist path that connects the entire Barangaroo precinct. It takes its name from the Aboriginal word for kingfish. The walk's northern end encompasses Barangaroo Reserve. The southern end passes many bars and restaurants and links to King Street Wharf.

③ Shell Wall

This seven-storey shell art installation is located at Barangaroo's southern gateway. Standing 22 m (72 ft) tall, the vertical series of aluminium shells represents the site's significant Aboriginal and maritime history.

④ Picnic on Stargazer Lawn

Climb the stairs to this gently sloping, 5,000-sq-m (53,819-sq-ft) elevated parkland for a picturesque picnic spot. It takes its name from Sydney Harbour's stargazer fish, which buries itself in the sand, eyes looking to the stars.

⑤ Barangaroo Ngangamay Rock Engravings

Hand-carved engravings by Aboriginal artists feature on five sandstone rocks throughout the reserve. The free dedicated app charts your location and reveals a wealth of information.

⑥ Flora

A key part of restoring the headland to its natural state was the planting of more than 75,000 native plants and shrubs to replicate the area's natural environment before European settlement. The species selected were largely indigenous to the headlands.

8 Aboriginal Cultural Tours

Aboriginal guides **(left)** take visitors on a journey through the history of the harbour and reveal the spiritual and cultural significance of the land to the heritage of the Gadigal people of Sydney.

MILLENNIA OF HISTORY

The land's traditional custodians, the Gadigal people lived in the area for more than 6,000 years. Settlements were located near the shoreline, with fish and shellfish the staple diet. Following colonization, as maritime activities and industry boomed, the headlands were whittled away to create wharves and a dockyard built by John Cuthbert. During the construction of Barangaroo Reserve, historic features were found and preserved, including a sandstone slipway from the 1820s and Cuthbert's sandstone seawall from 1865.

10 Shadows Art Installation

Artist Sabine Hornig's installation combines native plants, shadows and reflections on multi-coloured glass walls to create a botanical journey of discovery. The piece is installed across a 170-m (186-yd) walkway connecting the three International Towers.

7 Innovative architecture

In 2019 the precinct won the prestigious International Architecture Award for urban planning and landscape architecture. Notable buildings include the tri-level charcoaled-timber Barangaroo House *(see p47)* **(below)**, and the seven-storey, timber-built Damaru House.

9 Bird-watching

More than 150 bird species inhabit the Sydney basin and a wide array of birdlife is attracted to Barangaroo's abundant flora.

NEED TO KNOW

MAP L1–3 ▪ www.barangaroo.com

Aboriginal Cultural Tours: 10:30am Mon–Sat (90 minutes); adm

▪ For a casual and inexpensive waterfront meal, head to Belle's Hot Chicken restaurant *(5/33 Barangaroo Ave; www.belleshotchicken.com)* for Nashville-style fried chicken.

▪ The free Ngangamay Rock Engravings app uses augmented reality technology to reveal the area's Aboriginal history.

▪ While construction is still underway on central Barangaroo's attractions, visit the reserve as an extension of an excursion to the Rocks. For easy access to the southern precinct, take Wynyard Walk, a pedestrian tunnel running from Wynyard Station.

🔟 ⭐ Taronga Zoo

This zoo sits on 28 hectares (75 acres) of spectacular landscaped bushland with sensational views of the harbour. Originally located on "Billy Goat Swamp" in Moore Park in Sydney's east, Taronga opened in its current home in 1916. It cares for more than 4,000 animals and over 350 species, and undertakes research, conservation work and breeding programmes to protect and preserve wildlife and habitats. The zoo operates two wildlife hospitals, with over 1,400 admissions every year.

African Savannah ①

Perched high above Sydney Harbour, the giraffes **(right)** are one of the many African species at Taronga. The zoo is also home to meercats, hippopotamuses, zebras and barbary sheep.

② Rainforest Trail

Taronga's herd of Asian elephants is part of a breeding programme to protect the endangered species. Watch the young ones play and take a dip in their pool. Follow the leafy trail to see bongos, pygmy hippos and otters.

③ Sky Safari

Soak up the breathtaking harbour views from the Sky Safari cable car **(below)**, as it climbs up the hill to the zoo. Get a unique perspective as you watch the Asian elephants from above. The ride is included with admission.

④ Seal Walk

A 1.2-ha (3-acre) walk-through precinct houses Taronga's seals, sea lions, pelicans and penguins. The exhibit re-creates the animals' natural habitat with the glass-fronted enclosure revealing their movements to visitors.

⑤ Australian Walkabout

In this engaging exhibit visitors wander freely among kangaroos, wallabies and emus. At the Nightlife exhibit it is possible to spot bilbies, gliders and possums foraging in the dark.

⑥ Tiger Trek

Here you can come face to face with the critically endangered Sumatran tiger and find out how simple everyday shopping choices can help preserve its natural habitat.

7 Great Apes

At Taronga you can meet many of humankind's closest relatives, including gorillas **(left)**, orangutans and chimpanzees. The zoo is home to a large family of Western Lowland gorillas, which are criticially endangered in the wild, as well as one of the largest communities of chimpanzees outside Africa. Another primate highlight is the Lemur Walk, where you'll see ring-tailed lemurs at play.

8 Kids' Trail

The innovative Backyard to Bush exhibit melds the suburban home and the natural environment. Children can engage with farmyard animals at a small farm, while a wombat burrow gives a fascinating glimpse into the domestic life of these mammals. There's also a fun playground area, offering an opportunity for kids to blow off steam.

AUSTRALIAN SHARK ATTACK FILE

The zoo maintains the Australian Shark Attack File. The first recorded fatality was in 1791 on the north coast of New South Wales, the last in Sydney Harbour in 2022. Although shark attacks get a lot of press coverage, they are in fact extremely rare – prior to the tragedy in 2022, it had been 60 years since a fatality was recorded in Sydney. Beaches in the city are fitted with special shark nets, which are designed to reduce the chances of an encounter.

9 Reptile World

Some of the creatures here are stunning: the Komodo dragon, the red-eyed tree frog and the Fijian banded iguana for starters. More fear-inducing residents include Australia's taipan and the South American boa constrictor.

10 Koala Walkabout

As you stroll along this elevated path through the zoo, koalas **(below)** go about their main daily activities of sleeping and eating high up in the branches of eucalyptus trees.

NEED TO KNOW

MAP F2 ■ Bradley's Head Rd, Mosman
■ www.taronga.org.au

Open Sep–May: 9:30am–5pm daily; Jun–Aug: 9:30am–4:30pm daily

Adm (under 4s free; advance booking via the website is cheaper)

■ Arrive early as many animals are more active in the morning.

■ If you arrive by ferry, take the cable car from the bottom entrance to the top of the zoo and meander back down through the exhibits. It avoids the steep walk.

■ A zoo guide is available from the information desk near the entrance.

■ There are free talks and presentations during the day; check the website for details and times.

■ Experience a day in the life of a zookeeper with the Keeper for a Day programme.

■ Taronga has a range of food outlets including the 600-seat Food Market. The picnic area offers great views.

Bondi Beach

TOP 10 ⭐

Bondi may just be the most famous stretch of sand in the world. This glorious 1-km- (0.5-mile-) long sweep of golden sand is Sydney's favourite outdoor hub, packed with swimmers, surfers and people-watchers. But people come here as much for the trendy seafront cafés and cosmopolitan milieu as for the iconic beach – there's also a lively arts scene, with festivals, galleries, street art and more.

3 Surfing
It would be a shame to visit this famous surfing beach without at least trying to catch a wave **(left)**. The southern end of Bondi Beach is restricted to surfers; boards and wetsuits can be hired nearby. Get a lesson from Let's Go Surfing or Bondi Surf Co.

1 Bondi Beach Graffiti Wall
This collection of street art features constantly changing works by the best international graffiti artists. Each panel on the wall is allocated for a six-month time period before being reworked.

2 Sculpture by the Sea
This annual festival sees more than 100 artists install massive artworks along Bondi's wind-sculpted sandstone headlands. The exhibit runs from late October to November.

Bondi Beach

4 Ben Buckler
If you ever doubted the power of the ocean, check out the rock just below Ben Buckler, Bondi's northern headland. According to its brass plaque, this 240-tonne monster washed up during a storm in 1912. The nearby rock pool is great for children.

5 Swimming
The sand shelves off gently at the northern end of the beach, making it ideal for body surfing. Always swim between the flags. If the weather is on the wild side, leave the water to the surfers and enjoy the Coastal Walk instead.

BLACK SUNDAY
On 6 February 1938, three large waves rolled into Bondi Beach in quick succession. As they receded, hundreds of swimmers were swept out to sea in the backwash. By good fortune, almost 80 members of the Bondi Surf Bathers' Life Saving Club were gathered on the beach in readiness for practice rescues. Suddenly they were faced with the real thing. The life-savers rescued more than 250 people, although five swimmers drowned. The tragedy is remembered as Black Sunday.

6 Surf Life-savers

The people patrolling the beach in red-and-yellow caps are members of either Bondi Beach's Surf Bathers' Life Saving Club or North Bondi SLSC. These are two of the oldest clubs in Australia. Look out for the *Surf Life Saver* statue **(right)**, which is dedicated to the work of the surf life-savers.

7 Bondi Pavilion

This 1920s pavilion is the stylish home of a lively community cultural centre that hosts movies, theatre, workshops, free art exhibitions and a range of special events.

8 Bondi Icebergs

So named because its members swim throughout winter, this clubhouse is a Bondi institution. It's home to a decent restaurant and the world's only surf life-saving museum. Don't miss its clean saltwater pool.

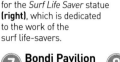

9 Campbell Parade

Bondi's main tourist drag **(left)** is always buzzing. Backpackers and tourists rub shoulders with supermodels, surfies and actors. It's a great place for gelati, fish and chips, or a beer overlooking the water.

10 Coastal Walk

This 5-km (3-mile) walk starts behind the Bondi Icebergs. Follow the path around to Tamarama Beach, also known as "Glamarama" for the glitzy locals. Further down the path is Bronte Beach, tiny Clovelly Beach *(see p56)*, Gordon's Bay and Coogee *(see p56)*.

NEED TO KNOW
MAP H5

Surfing: Let's Go Surfing, 128 Ramsgate Ave, North Bondi; www.letsgosurfing.com.au; Bondi Surf Co, 80 Campbell Parade, 0293 650 870

Bondi Pavilion: Queen Elizabeth Dr; www.waverley.nsw. gov.au

Bondi Icebergs: 1 Notts Ave, Bondi; open daily 11am–late Mon–Fri; 9am–late Sat–Sun; Icebergs Pool open Mon–Wed, Fri 6am–7pm; Sat–Sun 6:30am–7pm; closed Thu for cleaning; www.icebergs. com.au

■ It's a tiny spot, but the Crabbe Hole café on the pool deck at Icebergs is a great place for a good-value breakfast or lunch after a dip in the ocean pool *(thecrabbehole. business.site)*.

■ Watch films under the stars in the Pavilion's open-air courtyard. The annual Flickerfest short-film festival runs a varied programme for 10 days every January *(see p83)*.

The Top 10 of Everything

Waves lapping the golden sand at Bondi Beach

🔟 Moments in History

Contemporary cartoon of the arrest of Governor Bligh, 1808

① The Gadigal Arrive
The original settlers of Sydney Harbour, the Gadigal people, arrived almost 50,000 years ago. They fished in the summer months, and during winter they sought food inland and north towards the fertile Hawkesbury River valley. By the late 18th century, nearly 1,500 Gadigal people were estimated to live around the Sydney Harbour area.

② Captain Cook Lands
Aboriginal peoples living around Botany Bay encountered white men for the first time when Captain James Cook arrived at Botany Bay on 28 April 1770 and claimed the "Great South Continent" for Britain.

③ First Fleet Arrives
Governor Phillip and the First Fleet of 11 ships, carrying 1,500 convicts and staff, arrived at Botany Bay in 1788. Unable to find fresh water, Phillip sailed north to one of the world's "finest harbours". The establishment of a penal colony introduced diseases and conflict that decimated the Aboriginal population.

Captain Cook

④ Rum Corps
The disliked Governor Bligh threatened to curtail the privileges enjoyed by officers of the NSW "Rum Corps", who used liquor as a form of currency. They "arrested" Bligh as retaliation in 1808, but their coup was short-lived. Governor Lachlan Macquarie restored order in 1810 and went on to transform the penal colony into a town.

⑤ Troops Set Sail
The first of Australia's World War I volunteers set sail from Sydney Harbour on 1 November 1914, destined for battlefields in Europe and the Middle East. Almost 330,000 Australian troops served overseas and 60,000 died, which was the highest death rate per head of population of all the nations that were involved in World War I.

⑥ Builders' Labourers Impose Green Bans
Several areas, including the Rocks and Woolloomooloo, were saved from developers' wrecking balls in the 1970s. Fortunately for Sydney's future, the Builders' Labourers Federation imposed "Green Bans"

on projects that clearly threatened environmentally or historically significant buildings and precincts.

7 Mardi Gras is Born

Over 1,000 gay rights activists took to Sydney's streets demanding equal rights in 1978. Several protestors were arrested, but they vowed to return the next year. The parade that followed in 1979 established an annual event (see p82).

8 Reconciliation Walk

On 28 May 2000, more than 250,000 people walked across the Sydney Harbour Bridge to support calls for meaningful reconciliation between Aboriginal peoples and non-Indigenous Australians.

Cathy Freeman holding the flame

9 Cathy Freeman Lights the Olympic Flame

Aboriginal runner Cathy Freeman lit the Olympic flame to signal the start of the first Olympic Games of the new millennium in September 2000. Ten days later she became the first Aboriginal Australian individual Olympic gold medalist when she won the 400 metres.

10 Bushfires

The Australian bushfires of 2019–20 were some of the worst ever seen and devastated many parts of New South Wales. While Sydney was spared the worst, pockets of fire came within 15 km (9 miles) of the city centre and air quality was severely affected.

TOP 10 HISTORICAL FIGURES

Paul Keating

1 Pemulwuy
This Gadigal warrior resisted white settlement until he was caught and beheaded in 1802.

2 Barangaroo
This influential Aboriginal woman was leader of the Cammeraygal people of the Eora Nation at the time of European colonization.

3 John and Elizabeth Macarthur
The resourceful Macarthurs established Australia's agricultural industry in 1790.

4 Bungaree
He was one of the first Aboriginal people to act as a mediator between his own people and the government.

5 William "Billy" Blue
He started a ferry service between Dawes Point and the North Shore (see p127).

6 Wentworth, Blaxland and Lawson
Opening up Australia's interior, these European explorers crossed the Blue Mountains in 1813.

7 Caroline Chisholm
She arrived from Madras in 1838 to establish much-needed services for poor immigrant women.

8 Lilian Fowler
She became the first female mayor in Australia, after being elected mayor of Newtown in 1937.

9 Jack Mundey
Secretary of the Builders' Labourers Federation, Mundey led the Green Bans movement in the 1970s.

10 Paul Keating
Dubbed the "world's greatest treasurer", the former prime minister is an engaging commentator on Sydney heritage and development.

TOP 10 Architectural Highlights

1 Sydney Opera House

If you only manage to explore one building in Sydney, make it the Opera House (see pp12–15). The structure is not only beautiful from afar; a close look at the interior of the shells reveals the complexity of the gravity-defying design. Extensive modifications are currently underway to improve facilities and realize Jørn Utzon's original vision for the interiors.

2 One Central Park
MAP L6 ■ 28 Broadway, Chippendale

Designed by Pritzker-prize winning architect Jean Nouvel and best known for its vertical gardens, this skyscraper won the "Best Tall Building in the World" prize in 2014. The gardens cover 1,100 sq m (11,840 sq ft) and were designed by French botanist Patrick Blanc.

The hula hoop-like Exchange

3 The Exchange
MAP L5 ■ 1 Little Pier St, Haymarket

This is a spiralling, light-filled "hive" designed by the world-renowned Japanese firm of architects, Kengo Kuma & Associates. The Exchange opened in 2019 on the site of the former Sydney Entertainment Centre. Its six storeys are wrapped in sustainably sourced modified timber.

4 The Wharf Theatre at Walsh Bay
MAP M1 ■ Pier 4, 22 Hickson Rd, Walsh Bay

The heritage-listed Walsh Bay wharves were built out of brick and timber in the early 1900s as part of a port renewal programme. After the wharves fell into disuse in the 1970s, the establishment of the Wharf Theatre led to the area's transformation into a cultural hub.

5 Aurora Place
MAP N3 ■ 88 Phillip St

The ethereal white glass skin and sails atop Renzo Piano's office block and apartment buildings, built in 2000, echo the Opera House's shells and the spinnakers of yachts on the harbour. They also regulate the temperature, making the skyscraper one of the most energy efficient buildings in the CBD.

One Central Park

6 Governor Phillip Tower
MAP M2 ■ 1 Farrer Place

Part of a large development on a historic site, this elegant high-rise carefully slopes over several

19th-century terrace houses. The neighbouring Museum of Sydney (see p90) preserves the footings of the first Government House. In *Mission Impossible 2*, Tom Cruise abseiled through the steel blades in the roof of the Governor Phillip Tower.

7 Australia Square
MAP M3 ▪ 264–278 George St
▪ Adm

Built in the 1960s, this structure was a pioneering addition to Sydney's downtown, combining office, retail and public space. The building is still revered as a marvel of concrete construction. Architect Harry Seidler carefully softened the building's corners to reduce its shadow, giving the tower its iconic round form.

8 Rose Seidler House
MAP T2 ▪ 71 Clissold Rd,
Wahroonga ▪ 9989 8020 ▪ Open
10am–4pm Sun ▪ Adm

Commissioned by the mother of architect Harry Seidler, this was Sydney's most talked-about house when it was completed in 1950, assimilating the best Modernist features. Seidler launched his stellar career with this radical design that overturned almost every convention in suburban home design.

9 Barangaroo House
MAP L3 ▪ 35 Barangaroo Ave,
Barangaroo

This three-level circular structure features plant-covered balconies wrapped in timber and is one of the most popular dining destinations in Barangaroo (see pp36–7). The sculptural and three-dimensional

curving façade of the freestanding Barangaroo House has been likened to a spaceship and provides a fascinating architectural contrast to the towering skyscrapers that surround the building.

10 Dr Chau Chak Wing Building
MAP L6 ▪ 14–28 Ultimo Rd, Ultimo
Known locally as "the paper bag", the business school building at Sydney's University of Technology was designed by internationally renowned architect Frank Gehry and named for Australian-Chinese businessman and philanthropist Dr Chau Chak Wing. The building stands 41 m (134 ft) tall, with the façade being made up of 320,000 custom-designed bricks.

Dr Chau Chak Wing Building

⏱10 Museums

Rocks Discovery Museum

1 Rocks Discovery Museum

This small, free museum (see pp22–3) tells the area's stories and history through four permanent exhibitions. The exhibits cover the traditional custodians of the land, the impact of the establishment of the English colony, the city's port and maritime history, and the transformations in the area from 1900 to the present day.

2 Museum of Sydney

The Museum of Sydney (see p90) is located on the site of the first interaction between Sydney's Cadigal people and the British First Fleet. See what the city looked like 100 years ago and discover the history of its Aboriginal people.

3 Australian Museum

MAP N4 ▪ 1 William St ▪ 9320 6000 ▪ Open 10am–5pm daily ▪ www.australian.museum

Established in 1827, Australia's first museum is the place to explore the country's natural and cultural history through its huge collection of more than 21 million scientific specimens and cultural objects. It also houses 1,500 sq m (1,794 sq yd) of touring exhibition space.

4 Hyde Park Barracks Museum

MAP N4 ▪ Queens Square, Macquarie St ▪ Open 10am–5pm Thu–Sun ▪ Adm ▪ www.hydeparkbarracks. sydneylivingmuseums.com.au

Set in Francis Greenway's historic building, this museum (see p28) uses immersive audio technology to take visitors on a journey into the lives of the convicts, immigrants and Aboriginal peoples impacted by colonial Australia.

5 Australian National Maritime Museum

From Aboriginal watercraft to the history of the Royal Australian Navy, this collection of exhibits about life at sea has it all covered (see p35). It is possible to tour some of the historic boats moored nearby, including the replica of Cook's *Endeavour*.

One of the engaging exhibition spaces at the Museum of Sydney

occupied by residents until 1990. One of the houses has been re-created as a corner shop selling goods from the past.

9 Chau Chak Wing Museum

MAP C5 ■ University Place, opposite the Main Quadrangle, University of Sydney ■ 9351 2274 ■ Open 10am–4:30pm Mon–Fri, noon–4pm first Sat of the month ■ www.sydney.edu.au/museums

The University of Sydney's purpose-built museum includes the historic collections from its former Nicholson and Macleay Museums, as well as the University Art Gallery. There is an impressive collection of antiquities, including a large range of Egyptian and Eastern Mediterranean artifacts, and the vast entomological collection of the Macleay family.

10 Sydney Observatory

Part of the Museum of Applied Arts and Sciences, the Sydney Observatory (see p23) offers fascinating permanent exhibits and tours. Learn about the key role the observatory played in the history of timekeeping, meteorology and astronomy – during the 1880s, it became world-famous when the first astronomical photographs of the southern sky were taken here. There are interactive displays and games, and day and night tours include telescope viewing.

Sydney Jewish Museum

6 Sydney Jewish Museum

This foundation traces the history of Jewish life in Sydney, from a tiny group who arrived on the First Fleet in the 18th century to today's thriving community of over 30,000. There is also a Holocaust memorial and exhibit section, tours of which can be arranged (see p95).

7 Justice and Police Museum

Sydney's convict past was the start of a colourful history of crime and prosecution in the city. Find out about the gangsters of the past, the cops who caught them and Sydney's current underworld. The museum (see p90) features a vast collection of police and judicial evidence.

8 Susannah Place Museum

Built in 1844 by Irish immigrants, the terrace of four houses that makes up the Susannah Place Museum (p23) is as much a historic site as it is a museum. With the city's oldest original outdoor laundries and brick lavatories, this quaint row of small residences evokes life in early Sydney and was

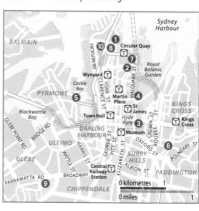

Art Galleries

An unusual exhibit at the White Rabbit Gallery

1 White Rabbit Gallery

This is one of the world's biggest and most significant contemporary Chinese art collections *(see p117)*, focusing on works produced post-2000. Two exhibitions each year are curated from the collection and presented over four floors.

2 Art Gallery of New South Wales

Sydney's most extensive art gallery *(see pp30–31)*, with a vast collection of modern and historical works.

3 Museum of Contemporary Art

A modern, cube-inspired extension sits beside the original 1950s mock Art Deco edifice, which housed the Maritime Services Board until it became a gallery in 1991. It is dedicated to exhibiting the work of contemporary Australian and international artists *(see p23)*.

4 Australian Design Centre

MAP N4 ■ 113 William St, Darlinghurst ■ Open 11am–5pm Tue–Fri, 10am–4pm Sat ■ www.australian designcentre.com

This centre exhibits works by textile designers, jewellers, glass-blowers, furniture makers and ceramicists, demonstrating crafts as real art forms. The store in the foyer has a range of limited edition pieces for sale.

5 Artspace

MAP P3 ■ 43–51 Cowper Wharf Rd, Woolloomooloo ■ 9356 0555 ■ Open 11am–5pm Mon–Fri, 10am–5pm Sat & Sun ■ www.artspace.org.au

This non-commercial collection presents contemporary works of traditional art forms such as painting, as well as experimental art through new media and performance.

6 Kate Owen Gallery and Studio

MAP B3 ■ 680 Darling St, Rozelle ■ Open 10am–6pm daily ■ www. kateowengallery.com

Spread over three floors, the Kate Owen Gallery displays and sells First Nations art by both established and emerging artists. Friendly and knowledgeable staff are on hand in the salons to answer questions.

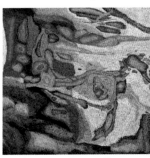

Painting at Kate Owen Gallery

Brett Whiteley Studio

When Brett Whiteley died suddenly in 1992, his wife turned his studio into a memorial *(see p102)*. The entire studio is now an adjunct of the Art Gallery of New South Wales (AGNSW), and Whiteley's bedroom and workspace have been left completely intact.

 S. H. Ervin Gallery

MAP M2 ■ 2 Watson Rd, Observatory Hill, The Rocks ■ Open 11am–5pm Tue–Sun ■ Adm ■ www. shervingallery.com.au

Enjoy a uniquely Australian art experience at one of Sydney's premier galleries. Housed in the historic headquarters of the National Trust of Australia, the gallery offers a wide-ranging programme of exhibitions and talks. Contributions made by Australian women artists are well represented.

 Tap Art Gallery

MAP N6 ■ 259 Riley St, Surry Hills ■ Open noon–6pm daily ■ www.tapgallery.org.au

Established in 1990 as an artist-run space, this gallery's uncurated approach means artists of all genres can exhibit their work. The result is a programme of diverse exhibitions.

State Library of New South Wales

State Library of New South Wales Galleries

Free rotating exhibitions in the library *(see p88)* are presented in six galleries. These cover paintings, photography, posters, monographs, ephemera and assorted historical material such as postage stamps, coins, architectural plans and sound recordings.

TOP 10 PUBLIC ARTWORKS

Edge of the Trees

1 Edge of the Trees by Janet Laurence and Fiona Foley
MAP N2 ■ Museum of Sydney
Symbolizes reconciliation with Aboriginal peoples.

2 Almost Once by Brett Whiteley
MAP N3 ■ AGNSW
Whiteley's sculpture of two matchsticks represents life and death.

3 40,000 Years Mural by Carol Ruff
MAP C5 ■ Lawson St, Redfern
A mural showing scenes from First Nations life over the last 40,000 years.

4 Veil of Trees by Janet Laurence and Jisuk Han
MAP N3 ■ The Domain
Ethereal images on glass reflecting light.

5 Magnolia & Palm by Bronwyn Oliver
MAP N3 ■ Royal Botanic Garden
Giant seeds recall early botanical studies.

6 Dual Nature by Nigel Helyer
MAP P2 ■ Woolloomooloo Bay
Whimsical structures play with the tides.

7 Wuganmagulya by Brenda L Croft
MAP P3 ■ Royal Botanic Garden
Celebrates the importance of this area of Sydney to Aboriginal peoples.

8 Memory is Creation Without End by Kimio Tsuchiya
MAP N3 ■ Tarpeian Way, The Domain
Sandstone blocks from demolished buildings lie on the grass.

9 Interloop by Chris Fox
MAP M3 ■ Wynyard railway station
Wooden escalators hang above their modern replacements.

10 Tied To Tide by Jennifer Turpin and Michaelie Crawford
MAP K2 ■ Pirrama Park
A dynamic sculpture.

TOP 10 First Nations Culture and Heritage

1 The Art Gallery of New South Wales

The Yiribana collection at the Art Gallery of New South Wales (AGNSW) includes traditional and contemporary work from First Nations communities across Australia *(see pp30–31)*.

2 Redfern Murals

MAP C5 ■ www.sydneyculture walksapp.com/barani-redfern

The First Nations peoples' civil rights movement found its home in Redfern in the 1960s. The area had been a gathering place for Aboriginal workers since the early 1900s. Two significant murals that highlight the heritage of the area are the *40,000 Years* mural opposite Redfern train station and *Welcome to Redfern*, a work covering what remains of a terrace house at 36 Caroline Street, created by Reko Rennie and draped in the colours of the Aboriginal flag.

3 Yabun Festival

MAP C5 ■ Victoria Park, Camperdown ■ www.yabun.org.au

Established in 2002 as an alternative Australia Day event, this festival celebrates First Nations peoples. It is the country's biggest one-day festival of Aboriginal culture, with performances, speakers, panels and stalls.

Rock art, Ku-ring-gai Chase NP

4 Ku-ring-gai Chase National Park

There are several rock art carving sites in Sydney that you can visit either on a tour or alone. The best examples are within Ku-ring-gai Chase National Park *(see p134)* in Sydney's north.

5 South Eveleigh Rooftop and Cultural Gardens

MAP C5 ■ 2 Davy Rd, Eveleigh ■ www.jiwah.com.au/projects

Australia's first Indigenous rooftop farm and a cultural landscape garden, co-designed with the local Aboriginal community, are located a short walk from Redfern station.

6 Garrigarrang: Sea Country

The Australian Museum's exhibition *Garrigarrang: Sea Country* has 300 rare and unique objects of the Sydney and NSW coastal communities *(see p48)*, including ghost net sculptures made from discarded trawler nets. The gallery explores First Nations culture, including Aboriginal creation stories, sustainability and conservation practices.

Yabun Festival

Badu Gili

This free six-minute projection on the Sydney Opera House sails is held four times a night. Meaning "water light" in the language of the Gadigal people, *Badu Gili (see p12–13)* highlights ancient Australian First Nations stories.

 Bangarra Dance Theatre
MAP M1 ■ Pier 4/5, Walsh Bay
■ www.bangarra.com.au

Established in 1989, this is one of the leading performing arts companies in the country. This Australian First Nations organization combines traditional storytelling with lively music.

9 Blak Markets
MAP U5 ■ www.blakmarkets.com.au

Held monthly at Bare Island, La Perouse, the Blak Markets offer a chance to experience the cultural practices of Aboriginal peoples and Torres Strait Islanders, including music and dance. You can also buy traditional art, crafts and bush foods.

Djaadjawan dancers at Blak Markets

10 Aboriginal Cultural Tours

There are several tours in the city offering a more structured introduction to Australian First Nations culture *(see p37)*. These experiences allow you to learn about a variety of subjects, such as bush food, medicine and the lives of Aboriginal people after colonization. Recommended tours include Dreamtime SouthernX, Royal Botanic Garden Aboriginal Heritage Tour, Barangaroo Headland Park and Kadoo.

TOP 10 INFLUENTIAL ABORIGINAL AUSTRALIANS

Actress Leah Purcell

1 Leah Purcell
Aboriginal Australian actress, director and writer; a Helpmann and AACTA Award winner.

2 Coleen Shirley Smith (Mum Shirl)
Co-founder of the Aboriginal Medical Service. A multilingual trailblazer who won numerous accolades for her work in First Nations peoples' health.

3 Pat O'Shane
One of Australia's great trailblazers, the first Aboriginal and female head of a government department.

4 Charles Perkins
Organized the Freedom Rides against segregation throughout NSW, later becoming a prominent public servant.

5 Stan Grant
A famous international journalist and later professor, best known for his First Nations peoples advocacy.

6 Stephen George Page
Artistic Director of the Bangarra Dance Theatre, a renowned Aboriginal contemporary dance company.

7 Anthony Mundine
Former rugby league player and boxer, named the Aboriginal and Torres Strait Islander Person of the Year in 2000.

8 Reko Rennie
A contemporary artist specializing in street art, winner of Australia Council's First Nations Arts Award.

9 Daniel Boyd
An internationally acclaimed artist who uses art to explore themes of colonialism and racism.

10 Linda Burney
Became the first Aboriginal woman to be elected to the Australian House of Representatives, in 2016.

🔟 Literary Sydney

Sydney Writers' Festival

1 Sydney Writers' Festival
www.swf.org.au

For one week in May, Sydney's biggest literary festival engages 100,000 attendees in a conversation about books and ideas. More than 300 events are held at venues that include Sydney Town Hall and City Recital Hall (see p72), and at the festival hub, Carriageworks, in the inner-city suburb of Eveleigh.

2 May Gibbs' Nutcote
MAP E1 ▪ 5 Wallaringa Ave, Neutral Bay; 9953 4453; open 11am–3pm Wed–Sun; adm; www.maygibbs.com.au

Nutcote was the home of children's author and illustrator May Gibbs, best known for her beloved gumnut babies Snugglepot and Cuddlepie. Situated above Neutral Bay, it is now a house museum on Sydney Harbour.

3 Sydney Writers' Walk
Etched with an excerpt of writing and a brief biography, the 60 bronze plaques that make up the Sydney Writers' Walk in Circular Quay honour local scribes such as Miles Franklin and Banjo Patterson.

4 Gertrude and Alice, Bondi Beach
MAP H5 ▪ 46 Hall St, Bondi Beach ▪ www.gertrudeandalice.com.au

With new and second-hand books piled high to the ceiling, this cosy bookshop and café is a haven for readers, writers and coffee drinkers.

5 BAD Sydney Crime Writers' Festival
www.badsydney.com

What can crime tell us about humanity? A panel of writers and reporters, detectives, psychologists and judges ponders the question each September during this three-day literary festival at the State Library.

6 The Bathers' Pavilion
www.batherspavilion.com.au

Raised on the Upper North Shore, *Big Little Lies* author Liane Moriarty – who has sold more than 14 million books worldwide – celebrates finishing each book she writes with a family meal at the restaurant in the 1920s pavilion on Balmoral Beach.

The charming cottage garden at May Gibbs' Nutcote

State Library of New South Wales

Dating back to 1826, Australia's oldest library *(see p88)* is a heritage-listed reference and research institution with many special collections. There are free exhibitions and author talks, along with several tours.

 Boundless Festival

MAP S4 ■ Bankstown Arts Centre ■ boundlessfestival.org.au
Celebrating culturally diverse Australian authors and writing in general, this free biennial festival includes author readings, panel discussions and workshops for both adults and children.

Boundless Festival

 Beatie Bow's Rocks

Ruth Park's popular children's novel *Playing Beatie Bow* sees a 14-year-old girl travel back in time to 1873, and is set in real-life locations in Sydney's historic the Rocks area. See what life would have been like then at the Susannah Place Museum *(see p23)*.

 Better Read Than Dead, Newtown

MAP B5 ■ 265 King St, Newtown ■ www.betterread.com.au
This three-storey bookstore in Newtown has been a literary landmark ever since it opened in 1996. The store hosts book club meetings for all ages, along with author events – don't leave without checking out the impressive art-works, on loan from the Corrigan Collection, on the third level.

TOP 10 BOOKS SET IN SYDNEY

Kate Grenville

1 The Secret River by Kate Grenville
In the early 19th century an Englishman is convicted of theft and sent to Australia.

2 The Harp in the South by Ruth Park
An Irish Catholic family lives and loves in mid-20th-century Surry Hills.

3 The Eye of the Storm by Patrick White
An ex-socialite in her eighties wreaks havoc on her family's lives.

4 Pemulwuy by Eric Wilmott
The biography of an Aboriginal man who led organized resistance against British invasion.

5 The Story of Danny Dunn by Bryce Courtenay
In the aftermath of the Great Depression, the popular son of a publican enlists to go to war.

6 Oscar and Lucinda by Peter Carey
Two 19th-century gamblers set out from Sydney to transport a glass church across the Australian wilderness.

7 Butterfly Song by Terri Janke
A young lawyer escapes Sydney for the home of her grandparents in the Torres Strait Islands.

8 Puberty Blues by Kathy Lette and Gabrielle Carey
Set in the 1970s, this is a raw coming-of-age tale of teenagers navigating life and Sydney's surf culture.

9 The Permanent Resident by Roanna Gonsalves
This collection of short stories describes the lives of Indian immigrants who come to live in Australia.

10 Looking for Alibrandi by Melina Marchetta
A tale of growing up in Sydney as the child of strict Italian immigrant parents.

Beaches

1 Bondi
MAP H5

Australia's most famous beach (see pp40–41) is a perfect crescent of sand with good surfing spots at either end, and usually calm enough for a swim in the middle. It's also got plenty of vibrant culture to explore beyond the shoreline.

2 Palm
MAP U1

The area around this beach is a magnet for Sydney's glitterati. "Palmie" is a lovely beach fringed by pine trees, and was made famous by the soap opera *Home and Away*. Take the short bush-walk at the northern end to Barrenjoey Lighthouse for great views.

3 Coogee
MAP U5

This is a relaxed beach with a busy vibe, popular with families and back-packers. There are headland parks, ocean pools and the Bondi to Coogee coastal walk for the energetic, as well as plenty of cafés.

4 Bronte
MAP G6

The picnic area at this small beach is dotted with little huts that provide picnic tables and shelter from the wind. At weekends it's packed with groups of 20-somethings and families enjoying barbecues and beer. Bronte also has a great ocean pool and a row of good cafés.

Bronte beach

5 Manly
MAP U3

On the peninsula's ocean side, this popular long beach (see p130) is the homeground of top surfers. The esplanade is good for jogging, and goes all the way round to lovely, sheltered Shelly Beach, which is great for snorkelling.

Surfer at Manly Beach

6 Clontarf
MAP U3

This harbour beach is wonderful for small children. There's plenty of shade, a playground, a shallow tidal pool and a great view of yachts moving to and from the marina opposite. After your swim, satisfy your hunger with a sizzling-hot plate of fish and chips at a beachside café at The Spit across the bay.

7 Nielsen Park
MAP G2

On summer weekends, this sheltered harbour beach is packed with picnicking families. The adjacent park (see p107) has good spots for cricket or frisbee. Small children can play safely in the water, but keep in mind that the harbour floor dips away suddenly.

8 Clovelly
MAP G6

If you walk between the cliffs that separate Bronte and Clovelly, you'll pass through Waverley Cemetery, the resting place of Aussie poet Henry

Lawson. Clovelly beach's waters are very calm due to its sheltered location, making it wonderful for children, laps and snorkelling.

Balmoral
MAP G1

Another excellent children's beach, Balmoral has a large enclosure of shark nets bordered by a wooden boardwalk that kids love to jump off. Grassy picnic areas abound here, the water is warm and calm, and there are many places to buy an ice cream.

Balmoral Beach

⑩ Maroubra
MAP U5

The Eastern Suburbs' most serious surf beach has big waves and a wide stretch of sand. When you're done with the water, walk round the coast to see a series of rock pools brimming with sea life. Maroubra offers good facilities such as a playground, changing rooms and a kiosk.

TOP 10 SWIMMING POOLS

Murray Rose Pool

1 Murray Rose Pool
Beautiful, large harbour enclosure. Tidal harbour pool (see p109).

2 Sydney Olympic Park Aquatic Centre
MAP S4 ▪ Olympic Boulevard, Sydney Olympic Park
Indoor water park for kids, with a superb range of facilities.

3 Maccallum Pool
A 1920s heritage seawater pool on the harbourfront (see p65), with waterside timber deck.

4 Andrew "Boy" Charlton Pool
Outdoor, saltwater pool in a picturesque setting (see p25). Sydney's style set love it.

5 Bondi Icebergs
Large outdoor pool. The home of winter swimming in Sydney since 1929 (see p41).

6 Dawn Fraser Baths
MAP B2 ▪ Fitzroy Ave, Balmain ▪ Open Oct–Apr
Outdoor tidal pool where the eponymous world record breaker got her start.

7 Wylie's Baths
MAP U5 ▪ Neptune St, Coogee
Popular ocean rock pool.

8 McIver's Ladies Baths
MAP U5 ▪ Beach St, Coogee
Coogee's women-only outdoor pool, in a secluded cliffside spot.

9 Fairy Bower
MAP U3 ▪ Bower St, Manly
Tiny ocean rock pool with incredible views over the Pacific.

10 North Sydney Olympic Pool
A historic Art Deco pool scenically located under the Sydney Harbour Bridge (see pp16–17).

Parks

Tabouchi trees in Centennial Park

1 Centennial Park
MAP F5

This is a gorgeous 189-ha (467-acre) expanse of playing fields, horse riding facilities (see p62), ornamental lakes and ponds, cultivated gardens, sports grounds, cycle and jogging paths, and light bushland with beautiful paperbark trees. It is the largest open space (see p101) in the central area and a popular barbecue and picnic spot.

2 South Head
MAP H1

In January 1788, Governor Phillip spent his first night in Sydney Harbour at South Head (see p107). The headland features the Hornby

Hornby Lighthouse, South Head

Lighthouse, painted in red-and-white stripes to distinguish it from the Macquarie Lighthouse. It's a prime vantage spot for viewing the Sydney to Hobart yacht race (see p83).

3 Lane Cove National Park
MAP S3

The park follows Lane Cove River, which flows into Sydney Harbour. Here you'll find echidnas, sugar gliders, mangroves, dusky moorhens, sheltered gullies and open eucalyptus forests with stately Sydney red gums (Angophora costata) growing out of the sandstone. At dusk their smooth pink bark is almost luminous.

4 Garigal National Park
MAP T3

This rainforest zone on the North Shore may offer you the best chance to spy the elusive lyrebird in its natural habitat. You will also find tree ferns and cabbage tree palms (Livistonia Australis), which were used by the Gadigal people to make fishing lines and thatched roofing.

5 Arthur McElhone Reserve
MAP Q3

Tucked below Kings Cross, this tiny manicured park is located in Elizabeth Bay (see p95). It features a stone bridge over a trickling pond filled with koi carp, and provides views of the yachts moored in Rushcutters Bay and the ritzy Eastern Suburbs enclave of Darling Point.

6 Bradleys Head
MAP F2

One of Sydney Harbour National Park's highlights is Bradleys Head, where you can often spot noisy flocks of rainbow lorikeets while walking on the trails. At the end of the headland is the tripod mast of the original HMAS Sydney (see p16) and a small Doric column marking one nautical mile from Fort Denison.

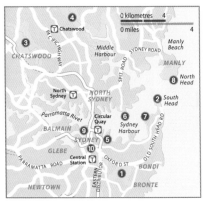

Collins Beach and the Old Quarantine Station (see p130). To the north are pretty Cabbage Tree Bay and Shelly Beach (see p130).

9 Observatory Park
MAP D3

Given its location beside the southern approach to the Sydney Harbour Bridge, this small park below the observatory (see p23) is surprisingly peaceful, with great views of the working harbour. Near the bandstand is a memorial to the Australians who served in the South African War (1899–1902).

10 Hyde Park
MAP N4

Situated on the edge of the city centre, this formal park (see p88) provides a respite from the city's bustle. It features a magnificent avenue of figs, the Art Deco Archibald Fountain and the Anzac Memorial (see pp88–9). A site for public executions up until 1802, Hyde Park was used for Sydney's first cricket match only one year later.

7 Nielsen Park
MAP G2

Overlooking Shark Beach and offering sheltered picnic areas and scenic walking tracks, this park (see p107) has been a Sydney favourite since 1912. Tucked amid the greenery on Steele Point Road is historic Greycliffe House. To the west is Steele Point, a former defensive battery.

8 North Head
MAP U3

This section of the Sydney Harbour National Park is more rugged than Bradleys Head, featuring windswept heathlands, shaded gullies, secluded

Archibald Fountain, the magnificent Art Deco centrepiece of Hyde Park

🔟 Walks

1 Bondi to Bronte
MAP H5

Part of the famous 6-km (4-mile) Bondi to Coogee walk, this 2-km (1.2-mile) stroll to Bronte Beach is perfect if you're short on time but keen to see some of Sydney's gorgeous coastline. The coastal path starts at the southern end of Bondi Beach and includes several sets of stairs. Highlights are Tamarama Beach and the historic Bronte Baths.

2 Watsons Bay
MAP H1

Officially the South Head Heritage Trail, this is an easy stroll from Watsons Bay Wharf to South Head. Along the way pass Camp Cove Beach where the First Fleet came ashore to meet with local Aboriginal people. Further along, the trail will deliver you to the candy-striped Hornby Lighthouse, on South Head.

3 Milsons Point, Kirribilli and Lavender Bay
MAP D2

This short 2-km (1-mile) walk offers some fantastic views of Sydney's most famous icons, including the garish smile of the Luna Park face. As you stroll along the waterfront to Lavender Bay, keep an eye out for a tunnel near the jetty and the stairs that lead up to Wendy's Secret Garden. The garden is an oasis that feels miles away from the rush of the city.

The rocky Hermitage foreshore

4 Hermitage Foreshore Walk
MAP G2

With undisturbed beaches and commanding harbour views, this 2-km (1-mile) track along shaded boardwalks leads you around a string of small coves, each more impressive than the last. The historic Strickland House and beautiful Milk Beach near the end of the walk are the jewels in its crown.

5 Long Reef Walk
MAP U3

This 3-km (2-mile) loop runs around the picturesque Long Reef Aquatic Reserve. It's also an excellent vantage point for whale watching between April and November, though if you are not lucky enough to spot one, you can snap a selfie with Kiah, a full-size baby whale sculpted from granite.

A section of the coastal Long Reef walk

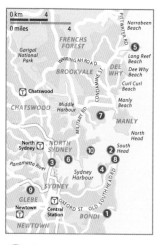

early years these cliffs claimed several ships. As a result, Macquarie Lighthouse, the first lighthouse in Sydney, was constructed.

9 Glebe Foreshore Walk
MAP K4

Starting at Sydney's fish market, this flat 4-km (2.5-mile) walk travels around the often-missed western side of the harbour. Passing the picturesque Blackwattle and Rozelle bays, the walk offers views of all three of the city's bridges: the Harbour Bridge, Anzac Bridge and Glebe Island Bridge. If you've worked up an appetite, continue to the Tramsheds – one of Sydney's hottest foodie destinations.

10 Taronga to Balmoral
MAP F2

This 6-km (4-mile) track is an "inner-city bushwalk", beginning at Taronga Zoo Wharf and following the harbour shoreline through Sydney Harbour National Park. Walk among Sydney red gums and past three serene harbour beaches before heading up to Georges Head Lookout. The walk rewards visitors with a wide variety of local birdlife, especially kookaburras and rainbow lorikeets. Upon finally reaching Balmoral, the hungry walker can choose from a variety of great dining options.

6 Cremorne Point Circuit
MAP E2

Cremorne Point Circuit is an easy 3-km (2-mile) walk through shaded bushland and past impressive waterfront mansions. Begin at Cremorne Point Wharf where you will find the historic Maccallum Pool, built by a local in the 1920s. Stay on the path to the lighthouse at Robinson Point and past the beautiful National Trust-listed Lex and Ruby Graham Gardens.

7 Spit Bridge to Manly
MAP U3

One of the longer walks in Sydney, this 10-km (6-mile) harbour track from Spit Bridge to Manly is challenging. But if you're willing to put in the effort the rewards are great, with 270-degree harbour views and six quiet harbour beaches. Grotto Point at Dobroyd Head features rock engravings etched into Sydney basin sandstone by the area's Aboriginal inhabitants.

8 Federation Cliff Walk
MAP H2

This 3-km (2-mile) walk provides the best views of the city's spectacular sandstone cliffs, standing 80 m (260 ft) high at the entrance of Sydney Harbour. In Sydney's

On the Taronga to Balmoral trail

🔟 Outdoor Activities

① Kayaking
Sydney Harbour Kayaks: MAP T3; 81 Parriwi Rd, The Spit Bridge, Mosman; www.sydney harbourkayaks.com.au
Get up close to Middle Harbour's mansions by kayaking with Sydney Harbour Kayaks. Discover hidden ecosystems on a guided tour or paddle around on your own, admiring the spectacular views as you go.

② Golf
Moore Park: MAP E5; Anzac Parade and Cleveland St; www.mooreparkgolf.com.au
There are some good public golf courses in Sydney. Moore Park is a championship 18-hole, par-70 course close to the CBD.

Golfers at Moore Park

③ Horse Riding
Eastside Riding Academy: MAP E5; Lang Rd, Moore Park; www.eastsideriding.com.au
Centennial Park has a showjumping area and an equestrian track that runs the 3.6 km (2.2 miles) around the park. Eastside Riding Academy offers escorted park rides and lessons in dressage and jumping.

④ Swimming and Surfing
Sydney has dozens of outstanding beaches and most are safe for swimming. The harbour beaches are generally calm, good for a relaxing paddle and for children. The ocean beaches *(see pp56–7)* receive more swell, which is ideal for surfing, bodyboarding and

Surfing at Manly

bodysurfing; you can take lessons at Bondi Beach with Let's Go Surfing *(see p41)*. At ocean beaches, make sure to swim between the flags, in the lifeguard-patrolled area.

⑤ Snorkelling and Diving
Dive Manly Centre: MAP U3; 10 Belgrave St, Manly; www.dive sydney.com.au
While Sydney's underwater world may lack the wow factor of Queensland's tropical reefs, it has its own draws, from dusky sharks to weedy seadragons. The sheltered bay at Shelly Beach in Manly is a popular spot for both snorkelling and diving, where you can hire equipment from the Dive Manly Centre.

⑥ Bushwalking
NPWS: www.nationalparks. nsw.gov.au
The bush is just a short train ride away from the bustling city centre. There are 24 national parks in and around Sydney, and all offer excellent bushwalks, organized by the National Parks and Wildlife Service (NPWS) for different levels of experience. Bushwalking – like hiking – is more strenuous than regular walking, due to the terrain and surrounding vegetation.

7 Ballooning
Balloon Aloft: www.balloon aloft.com
A dawn balloon flight over the Sydney region with Balloon Aloft is a tranquil yet exhilarating experience, offering lovely views of the sprawling city and the hazy Blue Mountains.

8 Sailing
Sydney Harbour Escapes: MAP B2; 2C Margaret St, Woolwich; www.sydneyharbourescapes.com.au
Charter a skippered yacht and relax as you sail around the harbour, or navigate in a 6-m (20-ft) cruiser.

9 Barefoot Bowls
Clovelly Bowling & Recreation Club: MAP G6; 1 Ocean St, Clovelly; www.clovellybowlingclub.com.au
Barefoot bowls (casual bowling) is a popular pastime in Sydney for young and old. Spectacularly positioned on the cliffs above Clovelly Beach, Clovelly Bowling & Recreation Club is the place to try it – or you can simply spectate with a cold beer in hand.

10 Cycling
Bonza Bike Tours: MAP M2; 30 Harrington St, The Rocks; www. bonzabiketours.com
There are cycle tracks across Centennial Park and in streets throughout Sydney. For a real cycling adventure, take a tour with Bonza Bike Tours along the foreshore and across the Harbour Bridge, or go further afield and mountain bike around the lovely Blue Mountains *(see p133)*.

Cycling in Centennial Park

TOP 10 SYDNEY SPORTING LEGENDS

Ian Thorpe

1 Ian Thorpe (b 1982)
Affectionately known as the "Thorpedo", the Sydneysider holds more Olympic gold medals than any other Australian.

2 Cathy Freeman (b 1973)
The Aboriginal sprinter's 400 m final win was the defining moment of the Sydney 2000 Olympic Games.

3 Donald Bradman (1908–2001)
The legendary cricketer used to travel 130 km (80 miles) from Bowral to Sydney every Saturday to play for St George.

4 Layne Beachley (b 1972)
Now the chair of Surfing Australia, this Manly surfer won the World Championships a record seven times.

5 Ken Rosewall (b 1934)
One of the greatest tennis players of all time, the octogenarian began playing at the age of three in Sydney's west.

6 Liz Ellis (b 1973)
The former Sydney Swifts captain is the most capped international player in Australian netball.

7 Jeff Fenech (b 1964)
The "Marrickville Mauler" is widely considered to be the best boxer Australia has produced.

8 Arthur Beetson (1945–2011)
In 1973, "Artie", who played for three Sydney clubs during his rugby career, became the first Aboriginal to captain Australia in any sport.

9 Dawn Fraser (b 1937)
From Balmain, Fraser is one of only three swimmers to have won the same Olympic individual event three times.

10 Tim Cahill (b 1979)
No soccer player has scored more goals for Australia than western Sydney-born Cahill.

🔟 Off the Beaten Track

① Wendy's Secret Garden
MAP D2 ■ Lavender St, Lavender Bay ■ Open 24 hrs ■ www.wendyssecretgarden.org.au

Following the tragic deaths of her husband, the artist Brett Whiteley, in 1992, followed by their actress daughter Arkie nine years later, Wendy Whiteley threw her energies into transforming the wasteland behind her house into a beautiful garden. This oasis, hidden among Lavender Bay Parklands, is one of the city's most serene green spaces and is still maintained by Wendy Whiteley herself.

② Bundeena
MAP T6

Surrounded by Royal National Park, the quirky village of Bundeena is reached by a short ferry ride from the southern Sydney beach suburb of Cronulla. It has many tranquil beaches, arty cafés and bushwalking opportunities, and it's worth the trip just to view the Aboriginal rock engravings at Jibbon Head, a 1.5-km (1-mile) walk east of town.

③ Bare Island Fort
MAP U5 ■ Bare Island Rd, La Perouse ■ Open Apr–Oct: 7am–7:30pm daily; Nov–Mar: 7am–8:30pm daily ■ www.nationalparks.nsw.gov.au

This tiny Eastern Suburbs island fort is reached via a 130-year-old wooden footbridge. Keen scuba divers and snorkellers take to

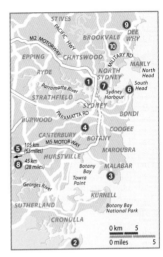

the water surrounding the island to explore local marine life. The fort was built in 1885 by British colonists convinced of an imminent Russian invasion.

④ Alexandria and Marrickville
MAP A6 & C6

As business owners continue to strike out further from the city's Central Business District (CBD) in search of affordable rents, the Inner West suburbs of Alexandria and Marrickville are having a foodie moment. Warehouses throughout the former industrial area have

Bare Island Fort

been transformed into destination cafés such as the Grounds of Alexandria, with Marrickville in particular offering some of Sydney's best inexpensive and diverse multicultural dining experiences.

5 Berrima
www.berrimavillage.com.au

Less than two hours' drive south of the city centre, the historic village of Berrima makes for a character-filled day trip. Widely recognized as the best-preserved Georgian village in mainland Australia, its streets are lined by colonial sand-stone buildings housing cafés, guesthouses and one of the nation's oldest licensed pubs.

6 Kutti Beach
MAP H2 ■ Wharf Rd, Vaucluse

Sydney is blessed with dozens of tranquil harbour beaches, yet most are well hidden. Accessed via a narrow, wooden stairwell in a residential area, charming Kutti Beach is one of the best concealed, making this thin strip of sand feel all the more exclusive.

7 Maccallum Pool
MAP E2 ■ Milson Rd, Cremorne Point ■ Open 24 hrs ■ www.north sydney.nsw.gov.au

Built in the 1920s and restored in 1985, this unique 33-m (108-ft) public swimming pool nestles below the waterfront mansions of Cremorne Point and boasts one of Sydney's best harbour views. The large timber deck is perfect for sunbathing and just lazing about.

Waterfalls in Dharawal National Park

8 Dharawal National Park
Victoria Rd, Wedderburn
■ www.nationalparks.nsw.gov.au

The neighbouring Royal National Park might be better known, but this park – named for its traditional custodians, the Dharawal people – is an equally lovely place to spend a day, with lookout points and walking tracks affording gorge and waterfall views. Pack a picnic and take the 1-km (0.5-mile) Jingga walking track to a beautiful swimming hole.

9 Dee Why
MAP U3

Often overlooked by visitors to the Northern Beaches, once-shabby Dee Why has smartened up. The seaside suburb now has one of the Beaches' best oceanfront café strips. There's also a 50-m (55-yd) ocean pool, and a scenic clifftop walking track to North Curl Curl Beach to the south.

10 Manly Warringah War Memorial State Park
MAP U3 ■ King St, Manly Vale ■ Open Apr–Oct: 7am–7:30pm daily; Nov–Mar: 7am–8.30pm daily ■ www.northernbeaches.nsw.gov.au

Known to locals as Manly Dam, this heritage-listed reservoir surrounded by bushland offers an easy outdoor escape for a change from beaches. There are four picnic areas and eight walking trails, including the 7-km (4.5-mile) circuit track that takes in several waterfalls and rock pools.

Children's Attractions

Children enjoying the State Library of New South Wales

1 State Library of New South Wales

The maze-like kids' space at the State Library of New South Wales *(see p88)* is devoted to young readers. Sit down and read some of the best children's books from Australian and international authors. There is a weekly story time for 3–5 year olds.

2 Luna Park
MAP D2 ■ 1 Olympic Dr, Milsons Point ■ Opening times vary, check website ■ www.lunapark sydney.com

Luna Park has been a Sydney harbourside icon and favourite since the 1930s. Modelled on New York's Coney Island, this amusement park is located on the North Shore, beside the Harbour Bridge. Enter through a 9-m (30-ft) clown face to enjoy classic attractions such as the dodgems and the Ferris wheel.

3 Australian Museum
The Australian Museum *(see p48)* is the perfect place for youngsters who are curious about the world around them, particularly when it comes to nature and culture. Kids' favourites include the giant 17-m (57-ft) whale skeleton suspended from the ceiling, cool fossils and the interactive Burra Learning Place. The museum runs themed activities that complement exhibitions.

4 Sydney Observatory
Take a tour with a real astronomer at Sydney Observatory *(see p23)* and peer through a historic telescope for an out-of-this-world experience. At night or twilight you'll get a close-up look at the moon, stars and planets, while during the day the solar telescope sheds a new light on the sun, stars, moon and Venus. Booking ahead is essential; check the weather first, as cloudy conditions limit viewing.

5 Centennial Park
This parkland *(see p101)* has three main attractions for kids: a designated cycle path near Alison Road, the equestrian centre *(see p62)* on Lang Road and the Ian Potter Children's Wild Play Garden, where kids can explore nature through creek beds, a water play area, bamboo forest and banksia tunnels.

Cycling in Centennial Park

6 Sydney Opera House

The Sydney Opera House (see pp12–15) hosts a year-round programme of shows tailored for children of different ages, especially during school holidays. Some shows include creative playtime and interactive installations for youngsters to engage with before and after performances.

7 Taronga Zoo

Taronga (see pp38–9) opened in 1916 in its idyllic harbourside location, with sweeping views across the water. The protection and preservation of endangered creatures is at the heart of the zoo's prolific conservation programmes. Free daily presentations include the engaging Free Flight Bird Show and a variety of keeper talks.

8 Shelly Beach

EcoTreasures: www.eco treasures.com.au

Snorkel straight off the sand at this sheltered, tranquil cove near Manly Beach (see p56). There's plenty to see underwater, including fish, rays and harmless Wobbegong sharks. Rent snorkel equipment and head out independently, or take a tour with an expert marine guide through EcoTreasures in Manly.

Fun at the Australian Maritime Museum

9 Australian National Maritime Museum

The Australian National Maritime Museum (see p35) runs Kids on Deck, a programme of creative activities for children aged 5 to 12. Kids might build their own ships or dress up in a costume, with events often linked to current exhibitions. There are also Mini Mariners sessions for preschoolers on Tuesdays.

10 Darling Quarter Playground

MAP L5 ■ Tumbalong Park, Darling Harbour ■ www.darlingquarter.com

This playground is one of the best in Australia. It has big slides, giant swings, a 21-m (69-ft) flying fox, a rope pyramid to climb, and water and sand play areas.

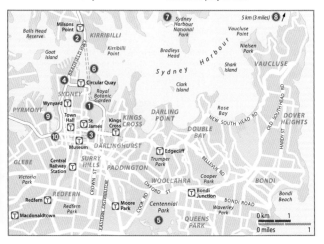

TOP 10 Performing Arts

Sydney Dance Company in action at the Roslyn Packer Theatre

 Sydney Dance Company

www.sydneydancecompany.com

With acclaimed dancers and guest choreographers, Sydney Dance Company has paved the way for the development of Australia's contemporary dance scene. The studio also runs daily dance classes for jazz, hip-hop and ballet, after which you can feast in the Sydney Dance Café.

 Sydney Symphony Orchestra

www.sydneysymphony.com

Based at the Opera House (see pp12–15), the Sydney Symphony Orchestra performs in the spectacular concert hall. The works played range from jazz and film soundtracks to classical orchestral masterpieces with the world's most illustrious conductors and soloists.

 Sydney Theatre Company (STC)

www.sydneytheatre.com.au.com

Sydney's premier theatre company performs regularly at the Roslyn Packer Theatre at Walsh Bay Arts Precinct and is also in residence at the Sydney Opera House (see pp12–15). The STC presents an exciting mix of classics and new Australian drama.

 Australian Brandenburg Orchestra

www.brandenburg.com.au

Australia's leading period music performers showcase their talent with a year-round programme of concerts at the City Recital Hall (see p72). The award-winning orchestra performs classical and baroque music from the 16th to 18th centuries, by composers such as Bach and Mozart, as well as less famous works by people like Corrette and Merula.

 Opera Australia

www.opera.org.au

Experience the energy and passion of the national opera company. The young singers and international stars of Opera Australia perform throughout the year at the Sydney Opera House (see pp12–15) – and occasionally on Sydney Harbour.

Opera Australia

6 Bell Shakespeare
MAP M1 ■ Pier 2/3, Walsh Bay
■ www.belleshakespeare.com.au

This is Shakespearean drama like you've never seen before. Since its foundation in 1990 by John Bell and Anna Volska, Sydney's theatrical blue-bloods, this company has presented the works of the Bard and modern classics in an accessible style.

7 Belvoir
MAP D5 ■ 18 & 25 Belvoir St,
Surry Hills ■ www.belvoir.com.au

Housed in the historic Belvoir Street Theatre, Belvoir has a well-deserved reputation for producing razor-sharp contemporary theatre. Its edgy, vital shows are always popular, especially with younger audiences.

Australian Chamber Orchestra

8 Australian Chamber Orchestra
www.aco.com.au

Daring programming and stylistic versatility set this chamber orchestra apart – and the fact that the violinists play standing up.

9 Ensemble Theatre
MAP D2 ■ 78 McDougall St,
Kirribilli ■ www.ensemble.com.au

Australia's longest continuously running professional theatre has nurtured the talents of the likes of Oscar-winner Cate Blanchett.

10 Bangarra Dance Theatre

This unique company *(see p53)* blends traditional Aboriginal and Torres Strait Islander history and culture with international contemporary dance. It is one of eight resident companies at the Sydney Opera House *(see pp12–13)*.

TOP 10 SYDNEY PERFORMERS

David Wenham

1 David Wenham
The critically acclaimed actor is at home in Sydney's Potts Point.

2 Russell Crowe
From his penthouse atop Finger Wharf in Woolloomooloo, the star of *Gladiator* and *Les Misérables* can enjoy water views.

3 Cate Blanchett
A graduate of Sydney's renowned National Institute of Dramatic Art (NIDA), the actress also ran the Sydney Theatre Company for four years with husband playwright Andrew Upton.

4 Toni Collette
A daring lead performance in *Muriel's Wedding* launched Sydney-born Collette on the world stage.

5 Rebel Wilson
Raised in suburban Sydney, the star of *Pitch Perfect* owns a waterfront home in Birchgrove.

6 Colin Friels
One half of a Sydney theatre power couple, Friels has performed in myriad stage and screen productions, often opposite wife Judy Davis.

7 Judy Davis
One of Australia's most respected actors, Davis has taken some of film's top honours; she lives in Balmain.

8 Nicole Kidman
Academy award-winning actor Kidman grew up and went to school in Sydney.

9 Hugo Weaving
A star of *The Matrix* and *The Lord of the Rings*, Weaving still calls Sydney home.

10 Bryan Brown
The iconic Aussie actor is often seen on Sydney's northern beaches.

🔟 LGBTQ+ Culture

1 The Red Rattler
MAP B6 ■ 6 Faversham St, Marrickville ■ Open for events; check website ■ www.redrattler.org

A charming and versatile warehouse theatre in Marrickville, the Red Rattler regularly hosts events, including parties, live music, cabaret and burlesque. The venue is run and operated by a group of artists and activists, so the events often have an explicitly political bent.

2 The Bookshop Darlinghurst
MAP N5 ■ 207 Oxford St, Darlinghurst ■ 9331 1103 ■ Open 9:30am–6pm Mon–Fri (to 7pm Fri & Thu), 10am–6m Sat, 11am–4pm Sun ■ www.thebookshop.com.au

All kinds of LGBTQ+ books and magazines are packed into this great shop, which covers everything from photography tomes to contemporary lesbian fiction.

The Bookshop Darlinghurst

3 Arq Sydney
MAP N5 ■ 16 Flinders St, Darlinghurst ■ Open 9pm–late Thu–Sun ■ www.arqsydney.com.au

One of Darlinghurst's most popular nightclubs, Arq is the perfect place to work up a sweat and dance the night away under lasers and strobe lights. It attracts a largely male crowd.

4 Imperial Hotel
MAP C6 ■ 35 Erskineville Rd, Erskineville ■ Open 4pm–late daily ■ www.imperialerskineville.com.au

Some of the classic drag show venues have closed down, but this

The Imperial Hotel

stalwart is still going strong. The hotel was featured in the cult film *Priscilla, Queen of the Desert*. There are shows most nights; check online for information.

5 The Bank Hotel
MAP B5 ■ 324 King St, Newtown ■ Open 10am–late daily (from noon Sun) ■ www.bankhotel.com.au

One of the more upmarket pubs on Newtown's King Street stretch, the Bank is popular for post-work drinks, with a great beer selection and food menu. The pub is spread across four floors, with a spacious beer garden at the bottom and Waywards, a busy live music venue, at the top.

6 The Beresford
MAP N6 ■ 354 Bourke St, Surry Hills ■ Open noon–midnight Mon–Wed, noon–1am Thu–Sun

The Beresford's Sunday sessions are among the busiest gay parties in Sydney, with some of the city's favourite DJs playing throughout the afternoon and into the night. It's also home to annual Mardi Gras events and hosts Bingay, a regular LGBTQ+ bingo night.

7 **The Bearded Tit**
MAP D5 ▪ 183 Regent St,
Redfern ▪ Open late daily ▪ the
beardedtit.com

A Redfern venue specializing in
queer art and inclusive good times,
the Bearded Tit hosts a programme
of curated visual and performance
art within the setting of a local bar.

8 **Toolshed**
MAP N5 ▪ Level 1, 81 Oxford St,
Darlinghurst ▪ Open 9:30am–1am
Mon–Sat, 9:30am–midnight Sun ▪
www.toolshed.com.au

An extremely popular adult store
and an institution among the
LGBTQ+ community for over three
decades, Toolshed offers novelty
adult shopping at its quirky best.

9 **Stonewall Hotel**
MAP N5 ▪ 175 Oxford St,
Darlinghurst ▪ Open noon–2:30am
daily ▪ www.stonewallhotel.com

Sharing the same name as New
York's Stonewall Inn, the spiritual
home of America's gay rights
movement, the Stonewall Hotel is
something of a similar landmark
for Sydney's gay community.

10 **The Oxford Hotel**
MAP N5 ▪ 134 Oxford St,
Darlinghurst ▪ Open 10am–3am daily
▪ www.theoxfordhotel.com.au

This is a great place for partying.
As well as its ground floor space,
the venue also includes Ginger's,
a swanky cabaret bar on the first
floor, and Polo Lounge, an elegant
bar and function space that can be
found on the second.

The Oxford Hotel

TOP 10 MARDI GRAS EVENTS

Mardi Gras parade performer

1 Festival
A month-long arts and cultural festival
(see p82) with dance parties, performing
arts, community and sports events.

2 Parade
Thousands attend the fabulous Mardi
Gras parade, the finale of the festival.

3 Party
Held after the parade, this is one of the
largest and most spectacular gay
dance parties.

4 Fair Day
Features stalls, music, food and a "Kids'
Zone", an area that offers activities for
children and their families.

5 Mardi Gras Film Festival
www.queerscreen.com.au
A great collection of global queer
cinema is screened over two weeks.

6 Sissy Ball
Interdisciplinary artist Bhenji Ra's
annual vogue ball is the biggest event
on Sydney's ballroom calendar.

7 Pool Party
Held on the rooftop of Ivy bar *(see p73)*
in the centre of the CBD, this party
always attracts a large crowd and some
of the city's best DJs.

8 Queer Thinking
This weekend of panels, workshops
and conversations tackles some of the
biggest issues facing queer people in
Australia and internationally.

9 LGBTQI + Elders Dance Club
This free community event champions
rainbow elders and gives them a
chance to dance.

10 Koori Gras
Queer First Nations artists are at
the centre of this packed programme
of performances.

🔟 Nightlife and Live Music

Performing at the Metro Theatre

1 Metro Theatre
MAP M5 ▪ 624 George St ▪ www.metrotheatre.com.au

Tiered levels of seating rising up to the bar at the back of the main room allow you to see the stage clearly from anywhere in the room. This and great acoustics make the Metro one of Sydney's best live music venues.

2 Home
MAP L4 ▪ 101/1–5 Wheat Rd, Darling Harbour ▪ www.home sydney.com

There's no place like Home. Since the opening-night performance by Paul Oakenfold, Sydney's only true superclub has been packed solid. The massive waterfront club features a multi-level main room with live music from the city's top DJs and an outdoor terrace. Attached to the main building is Homebar, a casual café and mellow bar. The hottest Sydney DJs have residencies at Home and top international acts are regularly featured on the bill.

3 Mary's Underground
MAP M2 ▪ 29 Reiby Place, Circular Quay ▪ www.marysunder ground.com

In a supper club-style setting a few minutes' walk from Circular Quay, Mary's Underground brings cabaret, rock'n'roll and old and new jazz performances to the city centre. A French-inspired bistro menu and darkened room make this a great place to spend a date night.

4 The Vanguard
MAP C5 ▪ 42 King St, Newtown ▪ www.thevanguard.com.au

Neon lights and live music performances, including burlesque, cabaret, blues and rock, are offered on most nights at the Vanguard. Rock to the beat from the comfort of a reserved table by choosing one of the dinner-and-show packages.

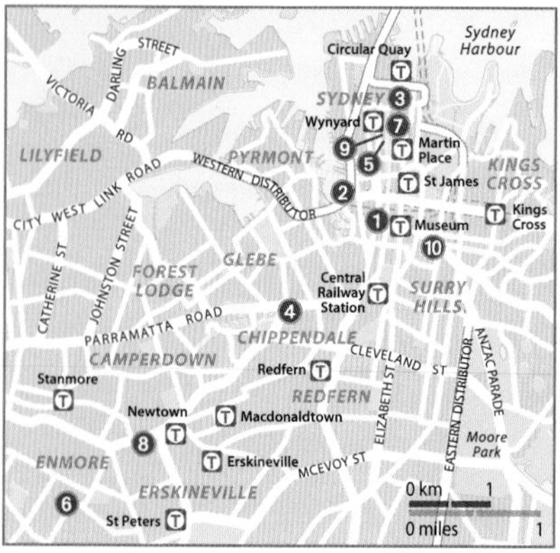

5 City Recital Hall
MAP M3 ▪ 2 Angel Place ▪ www.cityrecital hall.com

The first venue to be specifically designed for concerts built in Sydney since the Opera House, the 1973 City Recital Hall is an uplifting space, ideal for acoustic music. The quality of sound has already attracted many of Australia's leading musical companies, including the Australian Chamber Orchestra,

Musicians at City Recital Hall

the Sydney-based chamber music string ensemble Musica Viva and the Sydney Philharmonic Choir.

⑥ The Factory Theatre
MAP B6 ▪ 105 Victoria Rd, Marrickville ▪ www.factorytheatre. com.au

Everything from live music to comedy and cabaret are on offer in this large converted factory space in the industrial streets of Marrickville. Food trucks provide the catering and a large outdoor bar is the perfect place to chill out between sets.

⑦ Hordern Pavilion
MAP E5 ▪ 1 Driver Ave, Moore Park ▪ www.thehordern. com.au

Affectionately known as the Hordern to generations of Sydneysiders, this cavernous space in the Moore Park entertainment precinct is a concert venue that has hosted a who's who of the big names in music, as well as the annual Mardi Gras parade after-party.

⑧ Enmore Theatre
MAP B6 ▪ 130 Enmore Rd, Newtown ▪ www.enmoretheatre. com.au

In the heart of Newtown's trendy entertainment district, this fully refurbished old theatre hosts a wide range of local and international music acts such as Florence and the Machine, Paul Weller and Richard Ashcroft, as well as comedy performances from stand-up artists like Wil Anderson, Lano and Woodley.

⑨ Ivy
MAP M3 ▪ Ivy Complex, 330 George St ▪ www.merivale.com.au

A massive urban watering hole with eight bars and cocktail lounges as well as a range of restaurants, all spread over three floors. This is a wonderful place to go for live music, and there's even a rooftop pool if you also want to go for a swim.

⑩ Oxford Art Factory
Offering a mix of local and international artists, Oxford Art Factory (see p98) has two intimate spaces that are perfect for getting up close to the performers. There is a good blend of established and emerging musicians, DJs and art exhibitions on the schedule.

Aussie surf rock band Hockey Dad performing at the Oxford Arts Factory

🔟 Pubs and Bars

Opera Bar, with magnificent views over the harbour

① Opera Bar
MAP N1 ■ Lower Concourse, Sydney Opera House ■ Open 11:30am–late daily (from 11:00am Sat & Sun) ■ www.operabar.com.au

Views don't come much better than the spectacular panorama of the harbour, Harbour Bridge and city skyline from the Opera Bar. Soak up the sun on the terrace during the day, or sip cocktails in the evening.

② Establishment
MAP M2 ■ 252 George St ■ Open 11am–late Mon–Fri, noon–late Sat, noon–10pm Sun ■ www.merivale. com/venues/establishmentbar

Resurrected from the burnt-out shell of an 1892 emporium, Establishment has a 42-m (138-ft) marble bar and designer decor. Upstairs, try the elegant Hemmesphere bar.

③ The Newport
MAP U1 ■ 2 Kalinya St, Newport ■ Open 10am–late daily ■ merivale.com/venues/thenewport

Considered the top drinking spot on the Northern Beaches, the Newport deck is the place to be – particularly at sunset when there's live music.

④ Poly
MAP N5 ■ 74–76 Common-wealth St, Surry Hills ■ Open 5pm–late Tue–Fri, noon–3pm and 5pm–late Sat ■ www.polysurryhills.com.au

Located in the Paramount House Hotel (see p149), this walk-in wine bar appeals to all-comers thanks to its everything-to-everyone vibe. The excellent food menu makes a great complement to the extensive wine list.

⑤ The Loft at Bungalow 8
MAP L3 ■ King Street Wharf, 3 Lime St ■ Open 4pm–1am Mon–Thu, noon–3am Fri & Sat, noon–1am Sun ■ www.bungalow8sydney.com. au/the-loft

A sophisticated bar, with spectacular views and good service, the Loft at Bungalow 8 brings distinctive style to the Darling Harbour precinct.

⑥ Cruise
MAP M1 ■ Level 1, Overseas Passenger Terminal, West Circular Quay ■ Open 11am–late daily ■ www.cruisebar.com.au

Cruise offers wonderful views of the Opera House. Downstairs is the sprawling bar, modern and stylish, while upstairs is the more intimate and chic Junk Lounge cocktail bar with table service and a food menu.

Ordering drinks at Cruise

7 Arthouse Hotel
MAP M4 ■ 275 Pitt St ■ Open 10am–late Mon–Sat ■ www.ahhotel.com.au

This city hangout has four cocktail bars and a decent restaurant, all arranged over three levels. The main bar, named the Verge, was once a chapel and features 19th-century stencilling and skylights. The Dome Lounge and Attic bar provide more intimate and tranquil surroundings.

8 Manly Wharf Hotel
MAP U3 ■ Manly Wharf East Esplanade, Manly ■ Open noon–late daily ■ www.manlywharf.com.au

If the large public bar with its communal tables and lively atmosphere is too hectic for you, head outdoors to the Jetty Bar to watch the sun set over the harbour, or hide away in the cocktail lounge. There is live music on Tuesday, Wednesday and Thursday evenings, and DJs play at the weekends.

Hotel Palisade's homely pub bar

9 Hotel Palisade
This historic hotel (see p149) is the ideal place to soak up the local "wharfie" environment of Millers Point. Combine good pub food with a refreshing ale on the ground floor, or head upstairs to the stylish Henry Deane cocktail lounge for dinner and drinks with expansive city and harbour views.

10 Bondi Icebergs
Come and join the locals to watch a Bondi sunset over a beer in the bar of the low-key Icebergs Dining Room (see p41). If you are hungry after your drink, the stylish bistro here has a great menu to choose from.

TOP 10 CRAFT BREWERIES

The Lord Nelson Brewery

1 The Lord Nelson Brewery
www.lordnelsonbrewery.com
Australia's oldest pub brewery produces award-winning natural ales.

2 4 Pines
This is an all-in-one brewery (see p130) split over two levels. Tours available.

3 Batch Brewing Co
www.batchbrewingco.com.au
Batch serves up experimental beers in a casual environment. Tours available.

4 One Drop Brewing Co
www.onedropbrewingco.com.au
South Sydney's first microbrewery is home to the popular Botany Bay lager.

5 Bitter Phew
www.bitterphew.com
A casual spot to enjoy a selection of local and international boutique beers.

6 Keg and Brew
www.kegandbrew.com.au
A three-storey pub featuring a rooftop bar. More than 50 beers on tap.

7 Willie the Boatman
www.willietheboatman.com
This characterful establishment offers beer enthusiasts drinking paddles, brew batches and a tasting menu.

8 Young Henry's Brewery
www.younghenrys.com
The cellar-door tasting service is a particular favourite at this brewery.

9 The Endeavour Tap Rooms
www.taprooms.com.au
Try the 12 creative vintage ales and meet the brewer too.

10 Wayward Brewing Co
www.wayward.com.au
Hidden down a laneway, this place has 24 taps of rotating craft beers.

🔟 Local Foods

1 Sydney Rock Oyster

A culinary jewel harvested on the east Australian coast, the Sydney rock oyster is small in size, but big on flavour; its deep, rich, lasting sweetness distinguishes it from other varieties like the larger Pacific oyster. Best enjoyed raw, freshly shucked with lemon and pepper, it's also served roasted or shallow fried.

2 Balmain Bug

Not a bug but in fact a flat, deepwater crustacean (named after the suburb of Balmain), these lobster-like creatures have a hard external shell that turns red when cooked. They're usually cut in half, drizzled with olive oil or butter, seasoned with salt and pepper, and cooked on a barbecue in their shell.

3 Lamington

This sweet treat – made of squares of sponge cake dipped in chocolate sauce and rolled in desiccated coconut – is widely regarded as Australia's national cake. Lamingtons are found in most Sydney bakeries, with some slicing the cakes in half to add a layer of jam and cream in the middle.

Avocado and tomatoes on toast

4 Smashed Avocado

Avocados are nutritious, delicious and plentiful in Sydney, where they feature as a breakfast staple on café menus. Smashed avocado is the most popular dish, with roughly mashed and seasoned "avo" served on toasted sourdough or other artisan bread, alongside added extras like crumbled feta cheese or cherry tomatoes.

5 Bacon-and-Egg Roll

The traditional British bacon-and-egg breakfast is given an Australian twist in Sydney, where fried bacon and eggs are served in a bread roll and topped with caramelized onion and lashings of tomato relish. This quintessential takeaway breakfast is widely available at cafés for a hearty meal on the move.

6 John Dory

A popular fish commonly found in the waters of Sydney Harbour, John Dory has delicate, white flesh, with a firm, flaky texture and a mild, slightly sweet flavour. It's a highly versatile ingredient, ideal for steaming, baking, pan-frying and deep-frying.

7 Sausage Sizzle

Come the weekend, barbecues fire up at markets, parks, sports grounds and stalls outside Bunnings hardware stores, as community groups across the city run sausage

Lamington cake squares

sizzle stalls as fundraisers. Affectionately known as "snags" or "sangers", the barbecued sausages come either wrapped in bread or served in a bread roll, doused in tomato, barbecue or mustard sauce.

8 Meat Pies
The savoury star at Sydney bakeries and a favourite at big sporting events, the classic pie is made with a shortcrust base and a rich beef-mince gravy. Popular variations include cheese, mushroom and curry. Food trucks and pubs often serve pies topped with mashed potatoes, peas and gravy.

9 Chicken "Parmi"
A perennial favourite on pub menus, what Sydneysiders call "parmi" or "parma" evolved from aubergine parmigiana in Italy. The local version features chicken schnitzel (or "schnitty") topped with Italian-style tomato sauce and melted cheese, and is typically served with hot chips and a cold beer on "parmi night" at the pub.

Chicken "parmi" with chips and salad

10 Burger with "The Lot"
There are hamburgers, and then there are hamburgers with "the lot". For those not satisfied with onion, tomato, lettuce and cheese as toppings, order the works at a Sydney burger bar and wrap your mouth around an offering that includes a fried egg, a ring of tinned pineapple and sliced beetroot.

TOP 10 DRINKS

Craft beer, Young Henry's Newtowner

1 Young Henry's Newtowner
In a city heaving with craft beer, this inner-city brew leads the hipster pack.

2 Flat White Coffee
The most popular style to order in a coffee-obsessed city where bean roasting is an art form.

3 Fresh Juice
Widely available, freshly squeezed juices and smoothies are blended from seasonal fruit and vegetables.

4 The Original Sydney Cider
Made from the freshly crushed juice of Australian apples, fermented with Champagne yeast.

5 Espresso Martini
The popular caffeine-fuelled cocktail that keeps Sydney night owls partying.

6 Archie Rose Native Botanicals Vodka
Locally handcrafted vodka, infused with local flavours.

7 Lemon, Lime and Bitters
Originally a solution to seasickness, this refreshing drink mixes lemonade, lime juice and bitters.

8 PS Soda
Craft soda handmade in Sydney; flavours include wattle cola, smoked lemonade and bush tonic.

9 Manly Spirits Co. Gin
Dry Australian gin made with foraged native botanicals, distilled in small batches on Sydney's Northern Beaches.

10 Gelato Messina Thick Shake
Forget the cone – choose three scoops of gelato from 40 flavours for a shake to savour.

TOP10 Sydney for Free

1 Royal Botanic Garden

Join a free guided walk *(see p24)* through this 30-ha (74-acre) oasis overlooking Sydney Harbour. This is the best way to learn more about this centuries-old heritage-listed site, which features more than 5,000 plant varieties. The walk includes an exploration of Aboriginal culture and its connection to the land.

2 Sydney Opera House Light Show

Visit the Opera House *(see pp12–15)* in the evening and scope out the famous landmark before taking in the *Badu Gili* ("water light" show) – a six-minute animated projection of Aboriginal and Torres Strait Islander art reflected on the famous sails. *Badu Gili* is best viewed from the landmark's Monumental Steps.

3 Walk Across Sydney Harbour Bridge

MAP M1 ■ 100 Cumberland St

Take the stairs or lift to the pedestrian walkway of the Sydney Harbour Bridge *(see pp16–17)* and stroll across this iconic landmark while taking in the views and noise of the city. It takes about 30 minutes to walk the length of the bridge.

Walking across Sydney Harbour Bridge

Free Tours Sydney walking tour

4 Free Walking Tours

Free Tours Sydney: www.freetourssydney.com.au ■ I'm Free Walking Tours: www.imfree.com.au ■ Inner West Self-guided History Tours: www.innerwest.nsw.gov.au

Discover the city on foot with one of the free walking tours. Free Tours Sydney's 2.5-hour "colonial walk in modern Sydney" takes in the Rocks and Circular Quay; I'm Free Walking Tours (2.5 hours) start at the Town Hall and move into the Harbour; while Inner West Council has five self-guided history tours.

5 Explore Royal National Park

Spend time in nature among the kookaburras, echidna and lyre birds and admire the protected area *(see p134)* that encompasses coastal cliffs, secluded beaches and plenty of bushland. Vehicle entry costs $12 but the vast park is then free to explore.

6 Free Museums

Museums Discovery Centre: www.maas.museum/museums-discovery-centre

For those interested in history, the Rocks Discovery Museum *(see p23)* offers free half-hour guided tours twice a day, covering the full span of

Previous pages Looking over the harbour from the Royal Botanic Garden

the area's history from its traditional custodians, the Gadigal people, to the present day. Further afield, the Museums Discovery Centre in Castle Hill – a storage site for the Powerhouse, Australian National Museum and Sydney Living Museums – is packed with treasures and free to the public at weekends.

 Hit the Art Trail
The Museum of Contemporary Art's permanent collection (see p23) is free to view, while at the Art Gallery of New South Wales (see pp30–31) almost everything is free – the Yiribana Gallery of Aboriginal and Torres Strait Islander art is a particular highlight. The smaller White Rabbit Gallery (see p117) allows visitors to peruse all of its extensive Chinese collection without having to pay.

8 Visit Cockatoo Island
Discover the UNESCO World Heritage Site that was a convict prison, dock and shipbuilding yard in the 1800s. The island (see p122) is free to explore and there is plenty to do, including self-guided walks, free picnic and barbecue areas, and a visitor centre, although you must pay a modest fee to get there on the ferry from Circular Quay.

9 Music at Lunchtime
Attend a free 45-minute lunchtime concert in Verbrugghen Hall at Sydney's prestigious Conservatorium of Music (see p27). Students from this premier music institution perform the sessions as part of an annual programme that includes free masterclasses and lectures.

 Recordings of TV Shows
That's the Ticket: www.thatstheticket.com.au
Be in the audience for a variety of popular Australian television shows including *The Voice Australia* and *Australia's Got Talent*. Sign up on the That's the Ticket website to watch the shows in person.

TOP 10 BUDGET TIPS

Opal Card

1 Save on Transport
www.transport.nsw.info/tickets-opal
Use an Opal card (see p142) to travel by public transport. A $20 minimum credit balance is required.

2 Last-Minute Tickets
www.lasttix.com.au/sydney
For last-minute tickets for local shows try the discount ticket site Lasttix.

3 Discount Card
gocity.com/sydney
The Go Sydney card provides big discounts on a variety of attractions.

4 Well-Priced Seafood
www.sydneyfishmarket.com.au
For a good selection of local seafood at affordable prices, visit the fish market.

5 Sydney Museums Pass
www.sydneylivingmuseums.com.au/sydney-museums-pass
This offers entry to multiple museums run by Sydney Living Museums for $35.

6 Stage First
www.sydneytheatre.com.au
Save by booking tickets to preview performances of new theatre shows.

7 Aussie Fare
www.harryscafedewheels.com.au
Try the famous beef pie with mushy peas, mash and gravy from the cart at Woolloomooloo for less than $10.

8 Art After Hours
Head to the AGNSW (see pp30–31) after 5pm on Wednesday for free access to exhibitions, entertainment and talks.

9 Airport to City for Less
www.transport.nsw.gov.au
Hop on the local 400 bus towards Bondi Junction and take the train from there.

10 Dip in Style
Take a swim in the famous old Bondi outdoor pool (see p41) for only $7 or head to nearby Bronte Baths for free.

🔟 Festivals and Events

Australia Day celebrations

1 Australia Day
Various venues ■ **www. australiaday.com.au** ■ **26 Jan**
Celebrating the arrival of Sydney's First Fleet, this national holiday sees Sydney ferries and tall ships competing in a race from the Harbour Bridge to Manly and back again. There are free concerts and performances across the city. While the day is a celebration for many, for First Nations people – and others – this day is known as Invasion Day.

2 Sydney Festival
Various venues ■ **www.sydney festival.org.au** ■ **Jan**
Time your visit to coincide with this month-long international extravaganza of music, theatre, visual arts, dance and more. Past performers have included Bjork, Nick Cave, David Byrne & St Vincent, Sir Ian McKellen, P J Harvey, the Steppenwolf Theatre Company, Vietnamese Water Puppets and Les Ballets Africains.

3 Gay and Lesbian Mardi Gras
Oxford St ■ **www.mardigras.org.au** ■ **Feb & Mar**
This carnival is more than just a street parade (see p71); it's so pop-ular that more than a quarter of a million people line the route. The parade naturally ends with a party, but there is also an energetic programme of associated events that celebrates the strength and diversity of LGBTQ+ Sydney (see pp70–71).

4 Sydney Writers' Festival
Various venues ■ **May**
The roll call at this week-long event (see p54) includes more than 200 local and international speakers, with the occasional Nobel Laureate thrown in for good measure. There are many panel discussions, master-classes, book launches and readings.

5 Vivid Sydney
Various venues ■ **www. vividsydney.com** ■ **Late May/early Jun**
Sydney bursts brightly into colour every night in late autumn and early winter, with light projections and installations on buildings throughout the city. Expect a programme of music and talks, too

6 NAIDOC Week
Various venues ■ **www.naidoc. org.au** ■ **Early Jul**
The National Aboriginal and Islander Day Observance Committee Week celebrates the survival of Torres Strait Islander and Aboriginal cultures. Regular events include a prestigious art award and prizes.

First Nations dancing at NAIDOC Week

7 Festival of the Winds

Bondi Beach ■ www.waverley.nsw.gov.au ■ Sep

Sydneysiders love their kites – and there's no better venue for a day of mass kiting than Bondi Beach (see pp40–41), site of Australia's largest kite festival. Highlights include live music, dance shows and workshops.

8 Rugby League Grand Final

ANZ Stadium ■ www.nrl.com ■ Oct

Although Australian rules football is hugely popular in Sydney, the locals still get excited when the teams from the National Rugby League battle it out. If you can't get a ticket, catch the action on the big screen at a local pub.

Rugby League Grand Final

9 Manly International Jazz Festival

Various venues in Manly ■ www.northernbeaches.nsw.gov.au ■ Oct

Australia's largest community-based celebration of jazz has been running for 30 years. Manly (see p130) gives itself over to jazz for the Labour Day long weekend (first Monday in October). There are performances held at outdoor venues such as the beachfront, and indoor venues such as St Mathews Church on The Corso.

10 Sydney to Hobart Yacht Race

www.rolexsydneyhobart.com ■ 26 Dec

Organized by the Cruising Yacht Club of Australia, this bluewater classic has been Australia's best-known yacht race for over 75 years. Crowds line the harbour to wave off the crews as they pass through the Heads (see p59) en route to Tasmania.

TOP 10 CINEMA EXPERIENCES

Open-air cinema

1 Openair Cinemas
www.openaircinemas.com.au
Outdoor screens pop up in parks and on the harbour over the summer.

2 Govindas
www.govindas.com.au
A relaxed experience. Kick off your shoes and lie in cushion loungers.

3 Golden Age Cinema and Bar
www.ourgoldenage.com.au
Classic and cult movies in the old screening room of the 1940s Paramount Picture building.

4 Sydney Film Festival
www.sff.org.au
Watch a wide range of films all day, everyday – for two weeks.

5 Skyline Drive-In
www.eventcinemas.com.au
Old-school drive-in with an authentic 1950s-style diner.

6 Palace Verona Cinemas
www.palacecinemas.com.au
Arthouse releases, world cinema and Australian independent films.

7 Night Owls Kids Films Festival
www.darlingquarter.com
Free family-friendly flicks under the stars at Darling Harbour in January.

8 Hayden Orpheum Picture Palace
www.orpheum.com.au
A Wurlitzer organ rises from the stage pit at this Art Deco venue.

9 Flickerfest
www.flickerfest.com.au
Australia's only competitive global film festival, held at Bondi.

10 Palace Norton Street Cinemas
www.palacecinemas.com.au
These cinemas host festivals of foreign films.

Sydney
Area by Area

Residential buildings and lush trees in Kirribilli on the North Shore

TOP 10 City Centre

The city centre is bounded by Circular Quay, the Rocks, the Royal Botanic Garden, the Domain, Central Station, Darling Harbour and Chinatown. Here lies the best of old and modern Sydney, with historic buildings standing alongside glass and timber skyscrapers as the fast-growing city increasingly builds up, not out. Home to Sydney's best shops, massive museums, and stylish bars and restaurants, as well as numerous offices, this area is always a hive of activity. But there are some quiet moments to be found among the hustle and bustle: trundling along George Street – the city's spine – on a red tram, and wandering around the blue waterfront playground of Barangaroo and the green oasis that is the Royal Botanic Garden and the Domain.

Statue, Chinatown

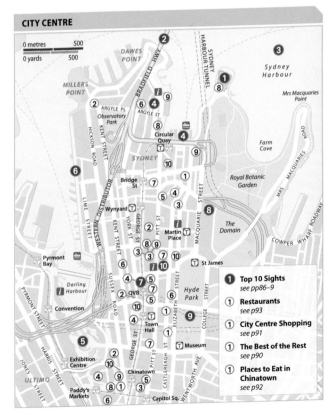

CITY CENTRE

1 **Top 10 Sights**
see pp86–9

1 **Restaurants**
see p93

1 **City Centre Shopping**
see p91

1 **The Best of the Rest**
see p90

1 **Places to Eat in Chinatown**
see p92

Sydney Harbour, the Harbour Bridge and Sydney Opera House

① Sydney Opera House

No trip to Sydney is complete without a visit to the masterpiece that is Sydney Opera House *(see pp12–15)*. It is Australia's most popular tourist attraction, as well as one of the world's busiest performing arts centres, hosting nearly 2,000 performances every year.

② Sydney Harbour Bridge

Prior to the construction of the Sydney Harbour Bridge *(see pp16–17)* in 1932, the only links between the city centre and the residential north side of the harbour were by ferry or a circuitous 20-km (12-mile) road route. The single-span arch bridge took eight years to build and is a spectacular sight in its own right, but particularly memorable views are granted by taking the BridgeClimb.

③ Sydney Harbour

Sydney's stunning harbour *(see pp18–21)* is a veritable aquatic playground, complete with beautiful beaches, lush parks and native bush habitats that offer countless walks and excursions.

④ The Rocks and Circular Quay

This part of Sydney *(see pp22–3)* is often referred to as the "birthplace of modern Australia", as it was here that the First Fleet landed in January 1788. Today, the historic cobbled streets of the Rocks and the busy ferry terminals at Circular Quay form part of the colourful promenade from the Sydney Harbour Bridge to the spectacular Sydney Opera House.

⑤ Darling Harbour and Chinatown

Darling Harbour's 1988 redevelopment transformed what was once an industrial centre into a lively low-rise tourism precinct *(see pp34–5)*. Neighbouring Chinatown is similarly bustling, with a mix of restaurants, food stalls and quirky gift shops.

⑥ Barangaroo

Barangaroo *(see pp36–7)* became Sydney's western harbour foreshore playground when a disused container terminal was transformed into a vast waterfront precinct. To the north, Barangaroo Reserve offers exceptional views, walking and cycling paths, and to the south are various entertainment spaces, bars, restaurants and boutique stores.

Cycling path at Barangaroo Reserve

QUEEN VICTORIA'S DOG

A statue of Queen Victoria and a wishing well stand at the Queen Victoria Building's main entrance. As you approach, a recorded voice recounts the story of Queen Victoria's favourite terrier, named Islay, who was "granted the power of speech" for helping deaf and blind children. And what a voice the dog has – Islay's story is told by none other than Sydney's "Golden Tonsils", retired radio shock-jock John Laws.

7 Queen Victoria Building
MAP M4 ▪ 455 George St ▪ Open 9am–6pm Mon–Sat (to 9pm Thu), 11am–5pm Sun ▪ History tours Thu & Sat, book via website ▪ www. qvb.com.au

The five-storey Romanesque Queen Victoria Building (QVB) staggers visitors with its beautiful tiled floors, elegant staircases, barrel-vaulted glass ceiling, copper-domed roof and stained glass. Built on the site of the old Sydney markets, this landmark structure was designed by George McRae and opened to applause in 1898. Today, the Queen Victoria Building houses local and international fashion brands.

8 State Library of New South Wales
MAP N3 ▪ 1 Shakespeare Place ▪ 9273 1414 ▪ Guided tours, call to book ▪ Adm ▪ www.sl.nsw.gov.au

This large heritage-listed reference and research library, first established in 1826, is the oldest in Australia. Open to the public, it holds more than five million items in its Mitchell and Macquarie Wings, built in 1910 and 1988 respectively. The huge exhibition spaces showcase this collection, and the library regularly holds a range of talks and events about history.

9 Hyde Park
MAP N4 ▪ Hyde Park ▪ 8262 2900 ▪ Open 9am–5pm daily ▪ Closed Good Fri, 25 Dec ▪ Guided tours, book via website ▪ www.cityof sydney.nsw.gov.au

A heritage-listed 16-ha (40-acre) park, this is the oldest public parkland in Australia. Mirrored in Hyde Park's Pool of Reflection is a 1934

Interior of the Queen Victoria Building

Art Deco monument built to commemorate Australia's World War I dead (see p44). It now records the sacrifices made by thousands of Australians in subsequent conflicts. The Hall of Memory is on the upper level, overlooking Raynor Hoff's moving statue, and the Hall of Silence is on the ground floor.

Anzac Memorial in Hyde Park

⑩ Sydney Tower

MAP M4 ■ 100 Market St
■ Open 10am–8pm daily (last entry 7pm, check website for variations in closing time due to special events) ■ Adm ■ www.sydneytowereye.com.au

Australia's 305-m (1,000-ft) icon offers 360-degree views over the Sydney region. The turret has revolving restaurants, a coffee shop and an observation deck. Above this is a 162,000-litre (35,500-gallon) water tank that acts as a stabilizer on windy days. The tower offers two attractions – Skywalk, an adrenaline-filled 45-minute guided walk around the glass-floored viewing platform outside the turret with incredible views of the city, and the 4D Cinema Experience, a virtual-reality ride across Australia with huge cinema screens and holographic imagery.

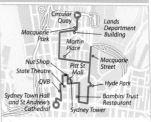

A WALK IN SYDNEY'S CITY CENTRE

▶ MORNING

From **Circular Quay** (see pp22–3) follow Loftus Street to **Macquarie Park**, where First Fleet HMS *Sirius* rests at anchor. Across the road is the 1876 **Lands Department Building**. Its façade features statues of explorers, including Ludwig Leichhardt. Head to **Martin Place** via George Street. Take a peek through the windows or inside the ornate former GPO and grand Bank buildings. Continue up Martin Place and turn left into **Macquarie Street** (see p28) towards Sir John Young Crescent where the State Library of NSW Mitchell Wing faces the Royal Botanic Garden. Head back along Macquarie Street to **Hyde Park** and its Art Deco Archibald Fountain. Wander the avenue of fig trees to Park Street. Turn right and snag a table for lunch outside the handsome **Bambini Trust Restaurant** at 185 Elizabeth Street.

AFTERNOON

Head to Market Street and turn left. **Sydney Tower**'s entrance and **Pitt Street Mall** are one and two blocks down on your right. Enter the mall and turn left into the Strand Arcade. Pick up handcrafted treats at the **Nut Shop**. Exit left at George Street and turn left into Market Street to peek inside the foyer and sweeping staircase of the **State Theatre**. Back on George Street, explore the wonderful architecture at the **QVB**. Exit from the York Street end and cross the road to **Sydney Town Hall** and **St Andrew's Cathedral**.

See map on p86 ←

The Best of the Rest

1 Museum of Sydney
MAP N2 ■ Phillip & Bridge sts
■ 9251 5988 ■ Open 10am–5pm daily
(to 8pm Fri) ■ Adm
This fascinating museum places the history of European settlement in the context of the Aboriginal custodianship of the land.

2 Martin Place
MAP N3
Martin Place runs from the General Post Office on George Street uphill to Macquarie Street. The 1891 GPO stands opposite the striking 1925 Neo-Classical National Australia Bank and the Cenotaph commemorating Australia's war dead.

3 Strand Arcade
MAP M3 ■ 412–414 George St ■ www.strandarcade.com.au
Designed by John Spencer and opened in 1892, this quiet and elegant arcade *(see p91)* is home to boutiques, jewellers, tailors, coffee shops and fashionable homeware stores such as Funkis and Dinosaur Designs *(see p91)*.

4 St Andrew's Cathedral
MAP M4 ■ Sydney Square
■ 9265 1661 ■ Open 10am–2pm Tue–Thu ■ www.sydneycathedral.com
Australia's oldest Gothic Revival cathedral was designed in 1868 by Edmund Blacket, who also designed St Stephen's *(see p117)*. It contains many memorials to Sydney pioneers.

5 State Theatre
MAP M4 ■ 49 Market St
■ 9373 6655 ■ Adm ■ www.state theatre.com.au
This theatre was originally a cinema with over-the-top Gothic, Baroque and Art Deco elements. Since 1974, it has been the premier venue for the Sydney Film Festival *(see p83)*.

6 The Great Synagogue
MAP M4 ■ 187a Elizabeth St, entrance on 166 Castlereagh St
■ www.greatsynagogue.org.au
With a picturesque location opposite Hyde Park, this is one of the world's finest synagogues.

7 Marble Bar
MAP M4 ■ 488 George St
■ www.marblebarsydney.com.au
The colonnaded entrance, mahogany counters, fireplaces and exquisite detailing make this heritage-listed venue the city's most impressive watering hole.

8 Museum of Contemporary Art (MCA)
Since it opened in 1991, this gallery *(see p23)* has acquired more than 4,000 contemporary and sometimes controversial works by Australian artists, spanning all art forms.

9 Justice and Police Museum
MAP N2 ■ Cnr Albert & Phillip sts
■ www.sydneylivingmuseums.com.au
This heritage-listed building was a water police station and courthouse that heard 17,000 diverse criminal cases every year in the 1880s.

10 Town Hall
MAP M4 ■ 483 George St
■ 9265 9189
The front steps of this elegant Victorian building with its fine clock tower have been a favourite meeting place for Sydneysiders for decades.

The striking St Andrew's Cathedral

City Centre Shopping

1 Castlereagh and King Streets

MAP M3 ■ Between Park St & Martin Place

Some of Sydney's most glamorous shopping is here, where you will find international labels such as Omega, Georg Jensen and Chanel.

2 Red Eye Records

MAP M3 ■ 143 York St
■ www.redeye.com.au

Sydney's best range of rock music and second-hand and rare records in an old-style music store. They also sell tickets to local gigs.

3 Dinosaur Designs

MAP M3 ■ Strand Arcade
■ www.dinosaurdesigns.com.au

The team behind this original jewellery and homewares shop are some of Australia's most celebrated designers. They craft their pieces from jewel-coloured resin.

4 Queen Victoria Building

MAP M4 ■ 455 George St
■ 9264 9209 ■ www.qvb.com.au

Over five levels, this heritage building houses the best of food, fashion, jewellery, art and antiques (see p88).

5 The Galeries

MAP M4 ■ 500 George St ■ 9265 6888 ■ www.the galeries.com

Shop for fashion, dine in the food court or browse at Books Kinokuniya, the largest bookshop chain in the southern hemisphere.

6 Market City

Situated above Paddy's Markets (see p35), this shopping centre contains an eclectic mix of local and international brands, including a range of quirky Korean clothes, electronics, discount shops and Asian food.

Westfield Sydney shopping centre

7 Westfield Sydney

MAP M3 ■ Pitt St between King & Market sts

Sydney's most expensive retail real estate space, offering six levels of chain stores and food outlets. It includes the Myer and David Jones department stores as well as a large number of designer boutiques.

8 Strand Arcade

The best of the Pitt Street arcades (see p90) houses gems such as Strand Hatters, the source of Akubra Aussie hats.

Andrew McDonald sign

9 Andrew McDonald Shoemaker

MAP M3 ■ Strand Arcade ■ 8084 2595 ■ www.andrew mcdonald.com.au

One of the few remaining shoemakers in Australia, Andrew McDonald has been hand-crafting elegant shoes for over three decades.

10 The Vintage Clothing Shop

MAP M4 ■ Shop 7, St James Arcade, 80 Castlereagh St ■ 9238 0090

Opened in 1976, this charming shop specializes in original, mint-condition vintage clothing for everyone. There is a smaller collection of high-end designer labels and accessories too.

See map on p86 ←

Places to Eat in Chinatown

1 Nanjing Dumpling
MAP L5 ▪ 6 Little Hay St, Haymarket ▪ 0499 333 808 ▪ $

Duck, dumplings and sesame rolls filled with pork and spring onions are the house specialities here.

2 Chinatown Noodle King
MAP M5 ▪ 1/357 Sussex St ▪ 9264 8890 ▪ www.chinatown noodleking.com ▪ $

A longtime Chinatown favourite dishing up generous servings of flavoursome homemade noodles, dumplings and congee in unpretentious surroundings.

3 Chat Thai
MAP M5 ▪ 20 Campbell St, Haymarket ▪ 9211 1808 ▪ www. chattai.com.au ▪ $$

A trailblazer that brought Thai food to Chinatown, leading to the creation of Sydney's adjacent "Thai Town" area.

Chat Tai dish

4 Xopp by Golden Century
MAP L5 ▪ The Darling Exchange, 1 Little Pier St ▪ 8030 0000 ▪ www.xopp.com.au ▪ $$

This restaurant is named for *XO pippies*, its signature dish. The Cantonese lunch and dinner menu is complemented by its *yum cha* offerings.

5 Boon Cafe
MAP M5 ▪ 1/425 Pitt St, Haymarket ▪ www.booncafe.com ▪ $

The restaurant is inside the Jarern Chai grocery store. Open for breakfast through dinner, it offers playful takes on Thai food, as well as other Southeast Asian cuisines.

6 Fortune Village
MAP M4 ▪ 209 Clarence St ▪ www.fortunevillage.com.au ▪ $$

Friendly, attentive service, comforting food and consistent quality for more than 30 years.

7 Mother Chu's Vegetarian Kitchen
MAP M5 ▪ 367 Pitt St ▪ 9283 2828 ▪ www.motherchusvegetarian.com. au ▪ $

Traditional dishes prepared by the Chu family, with Mama Chu still heavily involved. Order the vegetarian Peking Duck a day in advance.

8 Emperor's Garden Cakes and Bakery
MAP M5 ▪ Cnr Hay & Dixon sts ▪ 9281 5989 ▪ $

You won't get a better, budget-friendly dessert than the popular custard-filled pastry puffs served hot here, three for $1. Join the queue at the window to order or head inside and choose from egg tarts, buns and bakery treats.

9 Happy Chef
MAP M5 ▪ Shop F3, Sussex Centre, 401 Sussex St ▪ 9281 5832 ▪ $

This no-frills, hole-in-the-wall establishment in a food court is where you can order some of the best noodle soup and Malaysia laksa in town.

10 Mamak
MAP M5 ▪ 15 Goulburn St ▪ 9211 1668 ▪ www.mamak. com.au ▪ $$

Enjoy Malaysian food inspired by Kuala Lumpur's roadside stalls. You will know you've found it when you spot the queue.

Diners at Mamak restaurant

Restaurants

1 Alpha
MAP M5 ■ 238 Castlereagh St ■ 9098 1111 ■ www.238castlereagh.com.au ■ $$

A stylish setting matched by modern Greek food, full of flavour and designed for sharing.

2 The Lord Nelson Brewery Hotel
MAP L1 ■ 19 Kent St, The Rocks ■ 9251 4044 ■ www.lordnelson brewery.com ■ $$

The oldest continually licensed pub in Sydney, where punters have been enjoying good pub grub and a cold beer since 1841.

3 Rockpool Bar and Grill
MAP M3 ■ 66 Hunter St ■ Open Mon–Fri L & D, Sat D ■ www.rockpool barandgrill.com.au ■ $$$

Savour big-ticket cuts of beef and a pristine range of seafood from the sprawling menu at this handsome stalwart of a steakhouse.

4 Restaurant Hubert
MAP M3 ■ 15 Bligh St ■ Open Mon–Wed & Sat D, Thu & Fri L & D ■ www.restauranthubert.com ■ $$$

Enjoy superb French cuisine at this stylish and romantic restaurant. Try generous portions of timeless hits like textbook pâté and crème caramel.

5 Bentley Restaurant and Bar
MAP M3 ■ 27 O'Connell St ■ 8214 0505 ■ www.thebentley.com.au ■ $$$

Take advantage of the special lunch menu from Tuesday to Friday, to sample fine Australian food. You will receive excellent service in an industrial chic, moody space for much less than you would pay at dinner.

6 The Glenmore Hotel
MAP M2 ■ 96 Cumberland St, The Rocks ■ 9247 4794 ■ www.theglenmore.com.au ■ $$

Head straight up the three flights of stairs in this historic pub to reach the rooftop. Join the crowd soaking up the super harbour views over a "pub grub" meal and cold beer.

The rooftop at the Glenmore Hotel

7 Mr Wong
MAP M2 ■ 3 Bridge Lane ■ 9114 7317 ■ www.merivale.com ■ $$$

Cantonese-style food in which classic influences are given a contemporary makeover.

8 Bennelong
MAP N1 ■ Bennelong Point, Sydney Opera House ■ 9240 8000 ■ www.bennelong.com.au ■ $$$

Dine under the Opera House sails, where Australian ingredients and wines take centre stage.

9 Quay
MAP M1 ■ Upper level, Overseas Passenger Terminal, The Rocks ■ 9251 5600 ■ www.quay.com.au ■ $$$

The innovative flavours emphasizing native and unusual ingredients are incredible, the service impeccable.

10 Mary's
MAP M2 ■ 7 Macquarie Place, Circular Quay ■ 9002 0683 ■ Open daily ■ www.marys69.com ■ $

The meat-free counterparts are just as convincing at this top burger joint.

See map on p86

TOP 10 Kings Cross and Darlinghurst

Flower in the Botanic Garden

Sydney's largest red-light district is synonymous with strip clubs, tattoo parlours and nightspots, but nobody can deny that Kings Cross is the heart of the Inner East. Brimming with character, the area buzzes with visitors to its many cool cafés and hip wine bars. To the north, you'll find Potts Point with its historical villas and Victorian terrace houses and to the east the similarly upper-middle-class enclaves of Rushcutters Bay and Elizabeth Bay. The centre of Sydney's large LGBTQ+ community and the host of the city's epic Mardi Gras celebration every March, the high-energy region of Darlinghurst to the south guarantees great food and good times. To the west is East Sydney, with its "Little Italy" centred on Stanley Street, and to the north Woolloomooloo or "the Loo", a former docklands precinct known for its waterfront restaurants and classic pubs.

KINGS CROSS AND DARLINGHURST

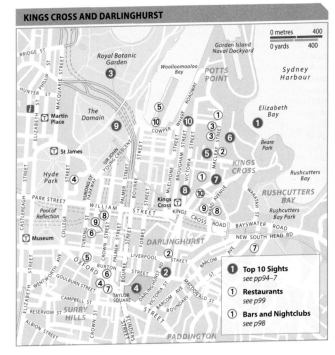

1	**Top 10 Sights**	see pp94–7
1	**Restaurants**	see p99
1	**Bars and Nightclubs**	see p98

A yacht moored at Elizabeth Bay

1 Elizabeth Bay
MAP Q3

Markedly more refined than Kings Cross, Elizabeth Bay's narrow, winding streets are packed with apartment buildings, including Art Deco gems such as Del Rio on Billyard Avenue, near Elizabeth Bay House. It is also home to several harbourside mansions, including Boomerang (see p19). The unpretentious Beare Park can be found just down the hill, on the harbour's edge.

2 Sydney Jewish Museum
MAP P5 ■ 148 Darlinghurst Rd, Darlinghurst ■ 9360 7999 ■ Open 10am–4pm Sun–Thu, 10am–3:30pm Fri ■ Adm ■ www.sydneyjewish museum.com.au

Following World War II almost 30,000 Holocaust survivors migrated to Australia, many of them settling in Sydney. This museum (see p49) explores Australian Jewish history through recordings of survivors, audio-visual displays and photographs. The ground floor deals with Jewish life within Australia, and the upper levels focus on the Holocaust, whose survivors act as guides.

3 Royal Botanic Garden and the Domain

A tranquil oasis in the heart of the city, the Royal Botanic Garden (see pp24–7) is Sydney's green lung. Its northern perimeter hugs the island-dotted harbour, making it the perfect place for a stroll. The grounds also house the Art Gallery of New South Wales (see pp30–31) and the Conservatorium of Music.

To the south is the Domain, an expansive grassy area that hosts everything from pulsating rock festivals to elegant open-air opera, quiet lunchtime joggers and raucous touch-football matches.

4 Darlinghurst Courthouse & Old Darlinghurst Gaol
MAP P5 ■ Courthouse: Taylor Square; open 10am–4pm Mon–Fri; www.supremecourt.justice.nsw.gov.au ■ Old Gaol: Forbes St; www.nas.edu.au

Mortimer Lewis designed the central section of this Greek Revival court-house in 1844, and James Barnet (see p109) designed the side wings in 1880. The 1841 Old Darlinghurst Gaol behind the courthouse was also designed by Mortimer Lewis and added to by James Barnet. In its early years, public hangings were conducted inside the gaol. In 1914 it became an internment facility for World War I "enemy aliens". It now houses the National Art School.

Old Darlinghurst Gaol building

5 Tusculum and Rockwall Villas

MAP P4 ■ Tusculum: 3 Manning St, Potts Point ■ Rockwall: 7 Rockwall Crescent, Potts Point

"Villa conditions" were actually established in the 1830s to ensure that the hillside overlooking Woolloomooloo Bay attracted the "right sort". All new houses had to face Government House (see p24), be approved by the governor of the day and be of high monetary value. John Verge designed both Tusculum and Rockwall. The Australian Institute of Architects now occupies the former. Rockwall is a private residence originally built for civil engineer John Busby, whose bore delivered Sydney's first permanent water supply.

6 Elizabeth Bay House

MAP Q3 ■ 7 Onslow Ave, Elizabeth Bay ■ 9356 3022 ■ Open 10am–4pm Sun ■ Adm ■ www. sydneylivingmuseums.com.au

Alexander Macleay, Colonial Secretary of NSW from 1825 to 1837, had architect John Verge design this residence for his large family in 1839. Macleay was also a distinguished botanist and the first president of the Australian Museum. This Greek Revival residence is said to contain the finest colonial interior on display anywhere in Australia. Macleay's family subdivided the original 23 ha (56 acres) of land following his death. In 1941 the house was further divided into 15 apartments. The property reopened as a museum in 1977.

A room in Elizabeth Bay House

Beautiful El Alamein Fountain

7 El Alamein Fountain

MAP Q4 ■ Fitzroy Gardens, Macleay St, Elizabeth Bay

A dandelion-shaped fountain in Fitzroy Gardens, El Alamein is particularly attractive when illuminated at night. Designed by local architect Robert Woodward in 1961, it commemorates the mass participation of Australian soldiers in the Battle of El Alamein in Egypt during World War II.

8 Victoria Street

MAP P3

This leafy stretch of Victorian terrace houses in Potts Point was a major flashpoint during the 1970s Green Bans (see p44). Pressure to demolish the terraces to make way for high-rise developments was resisted by residents and Juanita Nielsen, the local community newspaper publisher. On 4 July 1975, Nielsen attended a meeting at the Carousel Club in nearby Kings Cross; she was never seen again. Nobody in Sydney has any doubt as to the motive behind her murder.

9 Art Gallery of New South Wales

Established in 1871, the Art Gallery of New South Wales (see pp30–31) has occupied its present building since 1897. Today more than one million visitors a year enjoy the changing exhibitions, annual events

MR ETERNITY

During the Depression, Arthur Stace, a near-illiterate, reformed alcoholic, took to writing "Eternity" in perfect copper-plate script on pavements across the city, including on Victoria Street. Stace thought he had received instructions from God while he was at the Baptist Church in Darlinghurst, and he wrote the word "Eternity" half a million times before his death in 1967. A plaque for Stace can be found in Sydney Square.

and incredible collection, which includes modern and contemporary works, European and Asian pieces, colonial and contemporary Australian works and Aboriginal and Torres Strait Islander art. In fact, the Yiribana Gallery is one of the largest spaces in the world dedicated exclusively to Aboriginal and Torres Strait Islander art and culture.

The McElhone Stairs
MAP P3

Historically, the stone stairs linked the poorer working class of Woolloomooloo Bay with the well-to-do residents of Potts Point and The Cross. Further along Cowper Wharf Road is Harry's Café de Wheels, a Sydney late-night institution for more than 50 years, where locals and celebrities alike stop for pie and peas.

Climbing the McElhone Stairs

AN AFTERNOON IN KINGS CROSS

Begin at the **El Alamein Fountain**. Walk down Macleay Street and you'll pass the **Rex Hotel**, site of Sydney's first gay bar in the 1940s, the Bottoms Up.

Turn into Greenknowe Avenue and walk down the hill and left into leafy Ithaca Road, where you'll catch glimpses of the harbour. **Beare Park** is tucked between the high-rise apartments. From the wharf there's a very good view of **Boomerang**, the Neville Hampson-designed Spanish Mission mansion at Elizabeth Bay. Walk up Billyard Avenue to **Elizabeth Bay House**, passing the **Del Rio**, another Californian-style Spanish Mission building. Steps on Onslow Avenue will bring you back up the hill to Macleay Street.

Follow Cowper Wharf Road around to **Harry's Cafe de Wheels** for a "Tiger Pie" with mashed potato, mushy peas and gravy.

Turn left into Forbes Street for a pint at the historic **Tilbury** pub before making your way to Victoria Street via the **McElhone Stairs**. Turn left into Hughes Street and then Tusculum Street, and then right into Manning Street. Next door to **Tusculum Villa**, the Werrington and the Wychbury are some of the finest Art Deco buildings in The Cross.

On your way back up Macleay Street, pop into Orwell Street to see the old **Metro Theatre** (see p72), where a nightclub roared in the 1930s and rock concerts were staged in more recent times. Finish your afternoon tour with a reviving drink at the lively and elegant **Trademark Hotel**.

See map on p94 ←

Bars and Nightclubs

Outdoor seating at Dear Sainte Eloise

① Dear Sainte Eloise
MAP P4 ■ 5/29 Orwell St, Potts Point ■ 9326 9745 ■ www.dearsainte eloise.com

This European-inflected wine bar offers an affordable and extensive wine list, paired with Italian-inspired food.

② Darlo Bar
MAP P5 ■ 306 Liverpool St, Darlinghurst ■ 8587 4800 ■ www.darlobar.com.au

Soak in the retro atmosphere at this bar decorated with 1960s furnishings. The tables have old album covers scattered on top of them.

③ Ria Pizza and Wine
MAP Q3 ■ 71A Macleay St, Potts Point ■ 8080 9640 ■ www.riapizza.com.au

A wine bar and restaurant in a warmly lit industrial space. It offers sourdough pizzas with creative toppings.

④ Colombian
MAP N5 ■ 117 Oxford St, Darlinghurst ■ 9360 2151 ■ www.colombian.com.au

Enjoy people-watching as you sip a cocktail from a window seat or hit the dance floor at weekends.

⑤ Oxford Art Factory
MAP N5 ■ 38–46 Oxford St, Darlinghurst ■ 9332 3711 ■ www.oxfordartfactory.com

The After Dark Bar here is a meeting place for Sydney's art crowd. It's versatile, hosting everything from bands to computer game launches.

⑥ Shady Pines Saloon
MAP N5 ■ 4/256 Crown St, Darlinghurst ■ www.swillhouse.com

Behind an unmarked door in a dark lane, this American-themed saloon bar guarantees a rollicking good time.

⑦ Bitter Phew
MAP N5 ■ 1/137 Oxford St, Darlinghurst ■ www.bitterphew.com

Try the best local and international boutique beers in the beer garden here, or sit upstairs at the large bar.

⑧ Love Tilly Devine
MAP N4 ■ 91 Crown Lane, Darlinghurst ■ 9326 9297 ■ www.lovetillydevine.com

Named for the notorious Sydney brothel madam, Matilda Devine, this intimate laneway wine bar focuses on Australian winemakers producing organic and biodynamic wines.

⑨ The Long Goodbye
MAP N5 ■ 1/83 Stanley St, Darlinghurst ■ 8957 7674

Sip cocktails and listen to live music at this bar. If you can't decide on a drink, name a flavour and the staff will create a cocktail for you.

⑩ Dulcie's
MAP P4 ■ 44B Darlinghurst Rd, Kings Cross ■ www.dulcieskingscross.com.au

Step back into 1930s Sydney at this former basement strip club named for the era's "Queen of Bohemia".

Restaurants

1 Yellow
MAP Q3 ▪ 57 Macleay St, Potts Point ▪ 9332 2344 ▪ www.yellow sydney.com.au ▪ $$

Van Gogh-yellow walls and creative food make one of the most famous buildings in the Cross stand out at this bistro with modern European influences. Brunch is a must.

2 The Apollo
MAP Q3 ▪ 44 Macleay St, Potts Point ▪ ▪ $$

Opt for the "Full Greek" ($65) and sample the menu highlights of this modern Greek restaurant.

3 Cho Cho San
MAP Q3 ▪ 73 Macleay St, Potts Point ▪ www.chochosan.com.au ▪ $$

A Tokyo *izakaya* (informal Japanese bar) has been reimagined in this bright nook, where the small plates are as inventive as the cocktails.

4 Bodhi
MAP N4 ▪ 2–4 College St ▪ www. bodhirestaurant.com. au ▪ $

Expertly crafted dim sum and Taoist cuisine in leafy, idyllic surrounds.

Dim sum dish at Bodhi

5 Otto
MAP P3
▪ Area 8, Cowper Wharf Rd, Woolloomooloo ▪ www.otto ristorante.com.au ▪ $$$

A splashy, seaside Italian stalwart serving vegan and vegetarian tasting menus.

6 Dumplings & Beer
MAP N5 ▪ 83 Stanley St, Darlinghurst ▪ 9331 4905 ▪ www. dumplingsandbeer.com ▪ $

Styled as a retro Chinese teahouse, the original Potts Point outpost was a hit that spilled over into these larger premises in 2016. Expect the same menu of tapas-style snacks and beer.

PRICE CATEGORIES
For a two-course meal for one with a drink (or equivalent meal), plus taxes and extra charges.

$ under $50 $$ $51–120 $$$ over $121

7 Marta
MAP Q5 ▪ 30 McLachlan Ave, Rushcutters Bay ▪ 9361 6641 ▪ www. marta.com.au ▪ $$

This Italian restaurant is dedicated to *cucina romana*, complete with *pinza* (oval-shaped pizzas made with a lighter, more easily digestible dough).

8 Farmhouse Kings Cross
MAP Q5 ▪ 4/40 Bayswater Rd, Ruchcutters Bay ▪ 0448 413 791 ▪ www.farmhousekingscross.com. au ▪ $$

Tuck into the hearty set menu at Farmhouse and you'll feel like you are attending an intimate dinner party in a rural European home.

9 Sonora
MAP Q5 ▪ 37 Bayswater Rd, Potts Point ▪ www.sonora-mexican. com.au ▪ $$

Mexican-born chef Juan Carlos puts a creative and international twist on traditional fare at this distinctive desert-toned restaurant. The menu here is extensive and spans wagyu pastrami burritos to wild-caught sardines with avocado mousse.

10 Alibi
MAP P3 ▪ Ovolo Woolloomooloo, 6 Cowper Wharf Rd ▪ Open 4pm–late daily (from noon Sat & Sun) ▪ www.alibibar.com.au ▪ $$

Fun twists on familiar favourites are served here, with creative cocktails to match and eye-popping interiors to enjoy as you dine.

See map on p94

🔟 Paddington and Surry Hills

Once a largely working-class neighbourhood, Paddington underwent gentrification in the 1960s, as artists, students and young professionals were drawn to the area's cheap rents and pretty Victorian buildings. Now mostly white-collar families occupy the renovated terraces, and this hilly district, bordered by Centennial Park, Moore Park, Darlinghurst and the Eastern Suburbs, is one of Sydney's smartest addresses. Its main strip, Oxford Street, is a window-shopper's heaven and its backstreets are a delight for anyone who loves Victorian architecture. Surry Hills' charms took a little longer to be appreciated, but now this suburb rivals Darlinghurst and Newtown as one of the coolest districts in Sydney.

Oxford Street gables

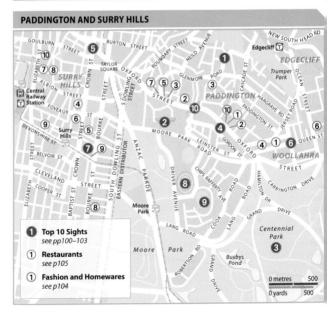

PADDINGTON AND SURRY HILLS

1 Top 10 Sights
see pp100–103

① Restaurants
see p105

① Fashion and Homewares
see p104

0 metres 500
0 yards 500

Victorian terrace house, Paddington

① Victorian Terrace Houses

Many of Paddington's lovely terrace houses, with their narrow frontages, ironwork verandas and pocket-handkerchief gardens, were erected following the construction of the Victoria Barracks in the 1840s. The area went into decline during 1931's Great Depression, but an influx of migrants revitalized the area after World War II. Many of those migrants moved out following the suburb's gentrification in the 1960s and 1970s.

② Victoria Barracks

MAP P6 ■ Oxford St ■ Open 10am–1pm Thu, 10am–4pm first Sun of the month ■ Army Museum: 9339 3330; open 10am–12:30pm Thu, 10am–4pm Sun; www.armymuseum sw.com.au

Occupying 12 ha (30 acres), these barracks were built between 1841 and 1848. They are immediately recognizable from Oxford Street by their high sandstone walls and many regard this complex of late Georgian buildings as one of the finest military barracks in the world. The architect was Major George Barney, who also designed Fort Denison. Until 1870 the barracks were home to British troops but today they are an Australian Army facility. The Army Museum is housed in the former military prison and contains several interesting exhibits tracing the military heritage of New South Wales. The Australian Army Band of Sydney is located at the barracks.

③ Centennial Park

MAP F5 ■ www.centennial parklands.com.au

More than 30 million people visit this historical and socially significant park. Originally a swamp, it became the water source for the city, then a public park, which opened in 1888. Covering 189 ha (467 acres), this tranquil urban green space includes formal gardens, ponds, avenues, sports fields and play-grounds. Heritage structures adorn the park, including the Federation Pavilion, the site of the Proclamation of Federation, which united Australia's six colonies as one nation. In 1901, more than 60,000 people gathered here to witness this event.

④ Paddington Markets

MAP E5 ■ 395 Oxford St ■ www.paddingtonmarkets.com.au

These markets are held every Saturday in the shaded grounds of Paddington Village's St John's Uniting Church. Ever since 1973, this alfresco bazaar has been a great place to shop for jewellery, crafts, fashion, pottery, soaps and second-hand clothing. It's always had a New Age bent, so you're also likely to find someone who can give you a massage, read your tarot cards or fine-tune your chakras.

A stall at Paddington Markets

An outdoor café on Crown Street

5 Oxford and Crown Streets

MAP N5

With its distinctive boutiques, Oxford Street is one of Sydney's most fashion-conscious shopping strips. Although it runs all the way from Hyde Park to Bondi Junction, the prime shopping drag is on the north side of the road between Barcom Avenue and Queen Street, which runs down to Woollahra. Surry Hills' Crown Street is less conspicuous and polished than its northern rival, but it's gaining a reputation as a good spot for homewares, retro and designer furniture and fashion items. It has some great cafés, multicultural restaurants and grocers, and pubs.

6 Queen Street

MAP F5

One of Sydney's most beautiful tree-lined streets, this is a peaceful haven for strolling and window shopping. Queen Street runs down between Oxford Street and Ocean Street, Woollahra; elegant terrace homes sit side by side with sophisticated small boutiques, exquisite modern homeware shops and design stores such as Alm. There are also a number of wonderful antique shops to explore, including Greene & Greene. A lovely independent bookstore – Lesley McKay's Bookshop – and numerous stylish cafés and restaurants all make this street well worth visiting.

7 Brett Whiteley Studio

MAP D5 ■ 2 Raper St ■ www.artgallery.nsw.gov.au

Tucked down a Surry Hills back-street, the former studio of maverick and controversial artist Brett Whiteley (see p51) is now a public museum and art gallery. Whiteley painted some of Sydney's most iconic works. He loved the harbour and the naked human form, and both feature in his paintings. In 1985 Whiteley converted this former factory into a studio but, just seven years later, he was found dead from a heroin overdose in a motel room in the south coast township of Thirroul. The gallery holds regular exhibitions and displays the artist's studio much as it was before he died.

8 Sydney Cricket Ground

MAP E5 ■ Moore Park ■ www.scgt.nsw.gov.au

When they were stationed at Victoria Barracks in 1851, the British Army were told to take their cricket bats and balls and entertain themselves on the empty land south of the barracks. Ever since then, this site has been the spiritual home for millions of cricket-loving Sydney-siders. In January 1928, fans saw Sir Donald Bradman – Australia's most famous cricketer – make his first-class debut here. The venue has also hosted concerts by the Rolling Stones, Madonna and Green Day, as well as Australian rules football and rugby league matches. Tours allow visitors into the dressing rooms and on to the hallowed turf.

Paddington Town Hall

9 The Entertainment Quarter

MAP E5 ■ Lang Rd, Moore Park
■ www.entertainmentquarter.com.au

This entertainment complex houses a variety of restaurants including Chinese, traditional Italian, cafés and modern Australian dining. Entertainment options include a large cinema complex, bowling, ski and snowboard simulators, go-kart racing, a Comedy Store and three pubs. There are two kids' playgrounds and two child entertainment venues. The Entertainment Quarter is also home to one of the best markets in Sydney, Cambridge Markets EQ, a lively gathering of farmers offering fresh seasonal produce and flowers. It is open from 8am to 2pm every Wednesday and Saturday.

10 Paddington Town Hall and Juniper Hall

MAP Q6 ■ 249 Oxford St

The Classical Revival Town Hall on Oxford Street was designed by J Kemp, a local architect who won an international competition to design a civic centre that matched the suburb's increasing status. The main building was completed in 1891, and the clock tower that now dominates was added several years later. Situated diagonally opposite the Town Hall, Juniper Hall was built in 1824 to house the 28 children from three marriages of Robert Cooper (1776–1857), notorious smuggler and Sydney's first gin distiller. The building's name derives from the berries Cooper used to make his gin.

A DAY IN SURRY HILLS AND PADDINGTON

> **MORNING**

From the Surry Hills Light Rail stop, head east on Devonshire Street to **Bourke St Bakery** for a takeaway coffee and pastry. Check out nearby **Brett Whiteley Studio**, before making your way to **Crown Street**. Window shop along here before turning right at Fitzroy Street, left into Hutchinson Street, and right into Albion Street. Cross Flinders Street, turn left to Moore Park Road and left again at Greens Road, with **Victoria Barracks** on your right, all the way to Oxford Street, Paddington. Pop into the **UNSW Galleries** on the corner before crossing the road for lunch at the delightful **Ampersand Café & Bookstore**.

AFTERNOON

After refuelling, head left along Oxford Street towards the intersection of Glenmore Road, home to a cluster of A-list designer boutiques. See the gallery spaces in 1840s terraces at **Maunsell Wickes Gallery** then continue along this winding thoroughfare to **Five Ways**, a quaint intersection surrounded by shops and pubs. Head up Broughton Street to the narrow laneway and steps on your left. At the bottom of the lane turn right and walk down to steep Cascade Street. Turn right and walk uphill past Windsor Street's incredibly narrow terraces to Paddington Street. Follow this avenue up to Jersey Road, home to the **Olsen Gallery**. Head down Halls Lane to reach elegant Queen Street and end your adventure with a drink at the **Woollahra Hotel** (116 Queen St).

See map on p100 ←

Fashion and Homewares

Products displayed at Alm

① Alm
MAP F5 ■ 118 Queen St, Woollahra ■ 9363 1459 ■ www.studioalm.com

Magnificently styled interior design store featuring an eclectic collection and splash of Mediterranean colour influenced by Alm's French origins in stylish St Tropez.

② Funkis
MAP Q6 ■ 202 Oxford St, Paddington ■ 9368 7045 ■ www.funkis.com

An Australian design company with strong Scandinavian influences, selling unique fabrics, clogs, fashion, jewellery and homewares.

③ Camilla
MAP P6 ■ 6/134–140 Oxford St, Paddington ■ 8021 5603 ■ www.au.camilla.com

Here, you can buy designer kaftans in vibrant colours and patterns and soft flowing lines characteristic of the designer's style.

④ Axel Mano
MAP F5 ■ 46 Queen St, Woollahra ■ 9362 3750 ■ www.axelmano.com

Locally designed and handmade bespoke hats, handbags, accessories and women's clothing are offered here. Most designs can be customized.

⑤ Scanlan Theodore
MAP P6 ■ 122 Oxford St, Paddington ■ 9380 9388 ■ www.scanlantheodore.com.au

A darling of the Sydney fashion scene for over 20 years, Scanlan Theodore offers simple yet elegant clothes made from a range of luxurious fabrics.

⑥ Pigott's Store
MAP F5 ■ 53 Ocean St, Woollahra ■ 9362 8119 ■ www.pigottsstore.com.au

Pigott's has a beautiful array of boutique furniture and accessories showcasing the Australian style with a touch of the Hamptons.

⑦ Zimmermann
MAP P6 ■ Shop 2, 2–16 Glenmore Rd, Paddington ■ 9357 4700 ■ www.zimmermann.com

Check out the great range of women's swimwear and gorgeous clothing.

⑧ Bev's Remnant House
MAP D5 ■ 722 Bourke St, East Redfern ■ 9310 1868 ■ www.bevsremnanthouse.wordpress.com

An extensive collection of fabrics for soft furnishings and upholstery. It also sells small homeware items.

⑨ Bourkeshire Interiors
MAP D5 ■ 631 Bourke St, Surry Hills ■ 0414 427 140 ■ www.bourkeshire.com.au

Interior design styling including cushions, fabrics and floor coverings.

⑩ Opus
MAP E5 ■ 1/354 Oxford St, Paddington ■ www.opusdesign.com.au

A Paddington favourite since 1968, brimming with a quirky mix of fun and fabulous items.

Restaurants

PRICE CATEGORIES

For a two-course meal for one with a drink (or equivalent meal), plus taxes and extra charges.

$ under $50 $$ $51–120 $$$ over $121

1 Saint Peter
MAP E5 ■ 362 Oxford St, Paddington ■ 8937 2530 ■ Open Tue & Wed D, Thu–Sun L & D ■ www.saintpeter.com.au ■ $$$
The seafood is exquisite, sustainably sourced and innovatively prepared, and the seven-course tasting menu changes daily.

2 Fred's
MAP E5 ■ 380 Oxford St, Paddington ■ 9114 7331 ■ Open Wed D, Thu–Sun L & D ■ www.merivale.com ■ $$$
Farm-to-table fine dining with an open kitchen and rustic country charm. The seasonal menu changes daily.

3 Tequila Mockingbird
MAP Q6 ■ 6b Heely St, Paddington ■ Open Tue–Thu D, Fri–Sun L & D ■ www.tequila-mockingbird.com.au ■ $$
Fresh and vibrant Latin American flavours served as tapas-style sharing plates. Get the tasting menu to try a bit of everything.

4 Bills
MAP N6 ■ 359 Crown St, Surry Hills ■ 9360 4762 ■ Open 7am–10pm daily ■ www.bills.com.au ■ $
Great all day, but go for breakfast to sample the legendary ricotta hotcakes with banana and honeycomb butter.

5 Nour
MAP D5 ■ 3/490 Crown St ■ Open Tue–Thu D, Fri–Sun L & D ■ www.noursydney.com ■ $$
Creative reimagining of classic Lebanese and other Middle Eastern flavours, including falafel crumpets, in a stylish space in Surry Hills.

6 Yulli's
MAP D5 ■ 417 Crown St, Surry Hills ■ 9319 6609 ■ Open daily D ■ www.yullis.com.au ■ $$
A long-standing neighbourhood spot for sharing plates of vegan and gluten-free food.

7 Bad Hombres
MAP M6 ■ 40 Reservoir St, Surry Hills ■ Open Tue–Sat D ■ www.badhombres.com.au ■ $
Reinvented Central and South American classics set to a rocking party-time soundtrack.

8 Firedoor
MAP M6 ■ 23–33 Mary St, Surry Hills ■ 8204 0800 ■ Open Wed–Sat D ■ www.firedoor.com.au ■ $$$
Open flames and burning embers bring out the brightness in a bevy of share-style dishes that change daily.

9 Porteno
MAP D5 ■ 50 Holt St, Surry Hills ■ Open Tue–Sat D ■ www.porteno.com.au ■ $$$
One for the meat lovers, this is Argentinian cooking at its finest.

10 Spice I Am
MAP M5 ■ 90 Wentworth Ave, ■ Open Tue–Sun L & D ■ www.spiceiam.com ■ $$
In a city of many Thai restaurants, this is among Sydney's best.

Lively Spice I Am restaurant

See map on p100

🔟 Eastern Suburbs

The Eastern foreshore of Sydney Harbour has long been a desirable place to live. Home to a mix of celebrities, politicians and middle-class families, the eastern suburbs offer idyllic harbour beaches, large parks and harbourside walking trails. Darling Point, Double Bay and Rose Bay feature million-dollar marinas and the most expensive real estate in the country. Away from the waterfront, the winding streets of Bondi, Bronte, Clovelly and Tamarama are full of homes with superb ocean views. These beachside villages offer an array of casual dining, fine restaurants and fashionable shops, as well as sea, sand and surf.

Macquarie Lighthouse

EASTERN SUBURBS

①	**Top 10 Sights** see pp106–109
①	**Restaurants** see p111
①	**Luxury Shopping** see p110

Lady Bay

Georges Head

Chowder Bay

Watsons Bay

Laings Point

Vaucluse Point

Shark Bay

Parsley Bay

Vaucluse Bay

Bradleys Head

Harbour

Diamond Hill

Sydney

Shark Island

Vaucluse

Clark Island

Woollahra Point

Diamond Bay

Piper Point

Blackburn Bay

Darling Point

New South Head Road

Dover Heights

Double Bay

Rose Bay

Royal Sydney Golf Course

Edgecliff

Bellevue Road

Victoria Rd

O'Sullivan Road

North Bondi

Edgecliff

Paddington

Woollahra

Cooper Park

Bellevue Hill

Old South Head Road

Blair St

Bondi

Oxford

Queen St

Street

Edgecliff Rd

Bondi Junction

Francis St

Cook Road

Lang Road

Centennial Park

Queens Park

Carrington Rd

Bondi Road

Tamarama

Marks Park

Ben Buckler

Bronte

0 km   1
0 miles   1

Sydney skyline visible from Camp Cove beach

1 Camp Cove and South Head
MAP H1

Just north of Watsons Bay is Camp Cove, where Governor Phillip spent the night after decamping from Botany Bay (see p44) and entered Port Jackson for the first time. A track leads from the kiosk at the northern end of this protected beach over to tiny male-nudist Lady Bay Beach, which is overlooked by the HMAS *Watson* Naval Base. At the end of the track is South Head's Hornby Lighthouse (see p58) and several old gun emplacements. This windswept headland offers spectacular views out to sea, across to Manly and the North Harbour.

2 Double Bay
MAP F4

This prestigious leafy area is home to some of the city's priciest residences. To the west is exclusive Darling Point, where you'll find Major Mitchell's former harbour side home on Carthona Avenue. To the east is Point Piper, which belonged to Sir Lawrence Hargrave from 1902 to 1915. In between is Steyne Park and the delightful Murray Rose Pool (see p109), just below the lovely Blackburn Gardens on New South Head Road. William Street, Bay Street and New South Head Road border the main shopping precinct, where you'll find all the best international retail stores.

3 Nielsen Park

Part of Sydney Harbour National Park, Nielsen Park (see p59) makes its way from the winding Vaucluse Road down to Shark Bay, so named for the marine life caught here in the days before shark nets. In the centre of the park is the Mt Trefle Walk, and near the beach are changing pavilions, the Arts and Crafts-style Greycliffe House and a memorial to the Harbour Foreshore Vigilance Committee (see p18). The Hermitage Foreshore Walk starts west of Shark Beach and offers some of the best views of Sydney as it meanders along the shoreline to Rose Bay via Hermit Point.

Greycliffe House, Nielsen Park

4 Vaucluse House

MAP H2 ■ Wentworth Rd, Vaucluse ■ 9388 7922 ■ Open 10am–4pm Thu–Sun, Jan: daily ■ Adm ■ www.sydneylivingmuseums.com.au/vaucluse-house

This property was built in 1803 and purchased by William Charles Wentworth in 1827. Wentworth was a major figure in the early colony – a barrister, explorer and statesman, he railed against the privileges enjoyed by the English-born colonists and lobbied for self-government. The Wentworth family lived in this Gothic house until 1861. It has been open to the public as a museum since 1910.

5 The Gap

MAP H1

This bluff, overlooking the ocean and the wave-lashed rocks far below, makes a spectacular lookout point over the South Head Peninsula. South of The Gap is the rusting anchor of the *Dunbar* and further south again is Jacob's Ladder: the sole survivor of the 1857 *Dunbar* tragedy was hauled to safety up this cleft in the rocks.

6 Watsons Bay

MAP H1

Known as Kutti to the Cadigal peoples, Watsons Bay was an isolated fishing village prior to 1860s development. On the waterfront of the bay near the ferry wharf, an inscribed stone seat commemorates the early 19th-century seaman who gave his name to this area. The imposing Greycliffe Memorial Gates, uphill from Robertson Park, were erected in 1929 in memory of the 41 lives lost in the Greycliffe ferry disaster of 1927.

7 Bondi Beach

When Bondi – which means "water breaking over rocks" in the Gadigal language – was declared a public beach in 1882, the crowds arrived and have never since gone away. The area *(see pp40–41)* saw significant development from 1920 to 1940, resulting in a strong presence of Art Deco and Spanish Mission architecture. After visiting the beach, take some time to explore the famous graffiti wall, Bondi Pavilion and the high street shops and cafés.

8 Macquarie Lighthouse

MAP H2 ■ www.harbourtrust.gov.au

Australia's longest continuously operating lighthouse stands on the windswept clifftops of Vaucluse. The original lighthouse, built between 1816 and 1818, was designed by noted convict architect Francis Greenway *(see p29)*. It was the first of many projects Greenway completed for Governor

Macquarie, earning him a conditional pardon. Within 60 years of its construction, the eroded tower was held together with iron bands and in 1883 a new lighthouse was designed by architect James Barnet (see p95) to closely resemble the original.

9 Rose Bay
MAP G4

The largest cove in Sydney Harbour is embraced by Point Piper to the west and Vaucluse to the east. Northeast of Point Piper is Shark Island (see p19). To the east is Hermit Point, reputedly the haunt of a reclusive former convict. In 1942 a Japanese submarine lobbed shells into Rose Bay, presumably aiming for the former flying-boat base; it's still the base for Sydney Harbour's seaplanes (see p20). If you have followed New South Head Road over from Double Bay, you'll enjoy the walk along the waterfront from Rose Bay Park to Lyne Park.

10 Murray Rose Pool
MAP F4 ■ New South Head Rd, Double Bay ■ www.woollahra.nsw. gov.au

Formerly known as Redleaf Pool, this tranquil harbourside tidal enclosure was renamed to honour Australian sporting legend and six-time Olympic swimming medallist Murray Rose. The golden sand, lush green grass, shady trees and kiosk facilities make it an ideal spot for a picnic and swim. The wraparound pontoon also makes for a lovely walk.

Dramatic ocean cliff, The Gap

A STROLL ALONG THE EASTERN FORESHORE

Lady Bay Beach
Camp Cove Kiosk
Camp Cove
Green Point
South Head
Watsons Bay Pilot Station
Watsons Bay Ferry Terminal
Shark Beach
Greycliffe House
Parsley Bay
Nielsen Park
Wentworth Mausoleum
Vaucluse House
BUS

▶ MORNING

Catch the 325 bus from **Circular Quay** (see p22) and get off at **Nielsen Park** (see p107). It's a short walk downhill to **Greycliffe House** and **Shark Beach**. When you're ready, walk back to Vaucluse Road, which becomes Wentworth Road. The entrance to **Vaucluse House** is further down on the right. Continue along Wentworth and take the first right into Chapel Road. WC Wentworth's gloomy mausoleum is just up the hill on your left. Steps lead from behind the mausoleum to Fitzwilliam Street. Turn right and walk downhill to the lane on your left, which takes you across the **Parsley Bay** suspension footbridge. Take the steps on your left leading up to The Crescent and follow this around until you reach Palmerston Street, which leads to **Watsons Bay Pilot Station**. Follow Marine Parade north to the **Watsons Bay Ferry Terminal**, where you can get fish and chips.

AFTERNOON

After lunch, walk to Short Street at the end of the beach, turn immediately left into Cove Street, and then left again into Pacific Street. This leads up to **Green Point** overlooking **Camp Cove**. After enjoying a swim here, or at the male-nudist **Lady Bay Beach** further on, follow the path along the clifftops to **South Head**. Have a snack at the **Camp Cove Kiosk** before retracing your steps to catch the ferry from Watsons Bay back to Circular Quay, or the bus from Hopetoun Avenue.

See map on p106 ←

Luxury Shopping

Chic clothing and homeware on sale at Commune, Bondi

1 Commune, Bondi
MAP H5 ■ 1/96 Glenayr Ave,
Bondi Beach ■ www.commune
bondi.com
This place, a few streets from Bondi
Beach, offers sustainable and fair-
trade handmade gifts, clothing,
jewellery and homewares.

2 Between the Flags
MAP H5 ■ 8/152 Campbell
Parade ■ www.betweentheflags.com.au
Take home a Bondi baseball cap,
beachwear, a tote bag or towel
as a souvenir from this shop.

3 Jan Logan
MAP F4 ■ 36 Cross St ■ www.
janlogan.com
Top-class jeweller Jan Logan offers
exquisite creations crafted from
precious and semi-precious stones.

4 Playa by Lucy Folk
MAP H5 ■ 3/11–13 Hall St,
Bondi Beach ■ www.lucyfolk.com
Along with Folk's playful jewellery,
accessories and range of sunglasses
handmade in Italy, Playa stocks
international designer clothing.

5 Tuchuzy
MAP H5 ■ The Beach House,
11/178 Campbell Parade, Bondi
Beach ■ www.tuchuzy.com
Shop for fashion and accessories from
the store's own brand, *Chosen by
Tuchuzy*, and international designers.

6 Belinda
MAP F4 ■ 8 Transvaal Ave,
Double Bay ■ www.belinda.com.au
Leading women's fashion boutique
Belinda stocks a mix of emerging
talent and high-end designers such
as Alexander McQueen, Missoni and
Victoria Beckham.

7 MUD Australia
MAP F4 ■ 1 Kiaora Lane,
Double Bay ■ www.mudaustralia.com
MUD's locally handmade porcelain
homewares come in a beautiful
range of colours and styles.

8 Coco and Lola
MAP F4 ■ 35 Bay St, Double
Bay ■ www.cocoandlola.com.au
A collection of women's Australian
fashion brands. Only the most
cutting-edge labels are stocked.

9 Bondi Wash
MAP H5 ■ 76 Gould St, Bondi
Beach ■ www.bondiwash.com.au
Buy sulphate-free, non-toxic
washing products that are made
using Australian botanicals including
wattle seed oil and lilly pilly extract.

10 Annex
MAP H5 ■ 8/178 Campbell
Parade ■ www.theannex.com.au
This Sydney-based contemporary
fashion label offers quality urban-
style menswear just metres from
Bondi beach.

Restaurants

PRICE CATEGORIES

For a two-course meal for one with a drink (or equivalent meal), plus taxes and extra charges.

$ under $50 $$ $51–120 $$$ over $121

1 North Bondi Fish
MAP H5 ■ 120 Ramsgate Ave, North Bondi ■ www.northbondifish.com.au ■ $$

Australian seafood is perfectly cooked by Matt Moran's team at this spot opposite the beach.

2 Empire Lounge
MAP G3 ■ Lyne Park, Rose Bay ■ www.empirelounge.com.au ■ $$$

Share plates, sushi and drinks are available in a beautiful harbourside setting. Request a table on the balcony and watch seaplanes take off from a nearby terminal.

Empire Lounge dish

3 Icebergs Dining Room
MAP H5 ■ 1 Notts Ave, Bondi Beach ■ www.idrb.com ■ $$$

Bondi's most iconic building serves modern Italian cuisine made with local Australian seafood.

4 Catalina
MAP G3 ■ Lyne Park, New South Head Rd, Rose Bay ■ www.catalinarosebay.com.au ■ $$$

Enjoy contemporary Australian cuisine with Italian and Spanish influences. The interior is elegant, and the views absolutely breathtaking.

5 Sean's
MAP H5 ■ 270 Campbell Parade, Bondi Beach ■ www.seansbondi.com ■ $$$

An institution for more than two decades, Sean's epitomizes the paddock-to-plate philosophy in dishes such as free-range roast chicken.

6 Charcoal Fish
MAP G3 ■ 670 New South Head Rd, Rose Bay ■ Open Wed–Sat ■ www.charcoalfish.com ■ $

Enjoy good-quality grilled Murray Cod dishes. Eat in or take away for a picnic at the nearby waterfront.

7 Lola's Level 1
MAP H5 ■ Level 1, 180–86 Campbell Parade, Bondi ■ www.lolaslevel1.com.au ■ $$

A small, stylish space with a southern European-inspired menu and signature cocktails.

8 The Botanica
MAP H2 ■ 2 Laguna St, Vaucluse ■ www.thebotanicavaucluse.com.au ■ $$

Try paddock-to-plate produce from New South Wales here.

9 Eden
MAP H5 ■ L106/180 Campbell Parade, Bondi ■ www.edenbondi.com ■ $$

Plant-based menu of shared plates and pizzas served in an outdoor dining area.

10 Indigo
MAP F4 ■ 6/15 Cross St ■ www.indigodoublebay.com ■ $$

Indigo offers modern Australian meals with a European twist, all-day breakfasts and healthy lunch options.

Inside the Indigo restaurant

See map on p106

TOP 10 Newtown and Glebe

The inner western suburbs of Newtown and Glebe, as well as adjacent suburbs Chippendale and Ultimo, together comprise a vibrant creative arts and education precinct on either side of Broadway and Parramatta Road. With three universities within walking distance, students rub shoulders with artists in the area's cafés, hip shops and small galleries. It is a great place to shop for funky clothes, books and retro furnishings, and it has some very cool cafés. Glebe, on the other hand, is a mix of gentrified residences at its harbour foreshore end and a hive of student and creative activity closer to Broadway. It is also home to numerous cafés and restaurants, book and antique shops, as well as pleasant harbourside parks and the ever-popular Glebe Markets.

Mosaic on a manhole cover

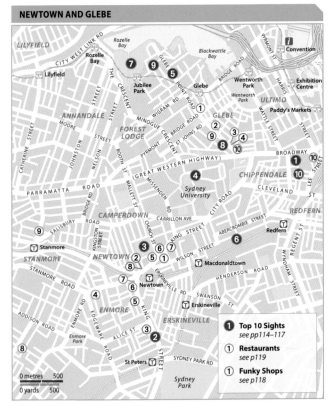

NEWTOWN AND GLEBE

1	**Top 10 Sights** see pp114–117
1	**Restaurants** see p119
1	**Funky Shops** see p118

Previous pages Waves lashing against The Gap near Watsons Bay

Vertical gardens at Central Park

1 Central Park
MAP L6 ■ 28 Broadway, Chippendale ■ 8123 4555 ■ www.centralparkmall.com.au

Occupying the site of a former brewery, this significant urban renewal project in the inner-city area includes a 6,500-sq-m (7,770-sq-yd) public park, retail outlets, galleries, entertainment facilities, restaurants and residential space, with award-winning architectural design including soaring vertical gardens.

2 King Street
MAP C5

Originally known as Cooks River Road, King Street has been an important thoroughfare since the days of European settlement, when it linked Sydney Town with farms in the Cooks River Basin. Newtown once belonged to a few rich men, but by the late 1800s it had become a thriving township. By then King Street looked much as it does today, bustling and lined with shops. Many stately homes on the streets off King Street have been restored, but most of the houses began as poor workers' cottages. Migrants arrived in the 1960s and 1970s, along with rockers, goths and punks, and Newtown is still peopled by an eclectic mix. Above the grungy street level, you will notice that the upper façades of many shopfronts have retained Victorian plasterwork detail.

3 Camperdown Cemetery
MAP B5 ■ Church St, Newtown ■ Open dawn–dusk

Sydney's oldest remaining cemetery lies in the grounds of St Stephen's Church. When the cemetery was established in 1848, it was one of three serving all of Sydney. Many historic figures are buried here, including Alexander Macleay (see p96), Colonial Secretary from 1825 to 1837. When the *Dunbar* sank just outside Sydney Heads in 1857 (see p108), the bodies recovered were buried in a mass grave at Camperdown and a memorial was erected for them. Eliza Donnithorne, thought to be the inspiration for Charles Dickens' Miss Havisham, also lies here. While walking the peaceful paths, note the gravestones lining the walls. These were moved inside the cemetary boundary when the outer area was turned into a park.

4 University of Sydney
MAP C5

Australia's first university was founded in 1850 and the Main Quadrangle building makes the site well worth a visit. Designed to mimic the hallowed halls of Oxford and Cambridge, its ornate Victorian Gothic façade is adorned with gargoyles and pinnacles. The more modern Chau Chak Wing Museum houses collections of art, antiquities and natural history (see p49).

Historic Sydney University building

⑤ Glebe Point Road
MAP J5

Glebe came about as a series of land grants to wealthy free settlers. Two remaining Regency villas, Toxteth Park and Lyndhurst, were designed by celebrated 19th-century architect John Verge. Today, the area is an enclave characterized by New Age and health-food shops and laid-back locals. Leafy and settled into hills with harbour views, the area has a village atmosphere. Glebe Point Road runs through the centre, from Broadway down to the water at Jubilee Point, and is lined with shops and cafés. Pop into Sappho bookshop and café, then head to the Toxteth pub for a cold beer and classic pub meal in the large outdoor area.

⑥ Carriageworks
MAP C5 ■ 245 Wilson St, Eveleigh ■ 8751 9099 ■ www. carriageworks.com.au

This impressive multi-arts centre is definitely one of Sydney's edgiest cultural precincts, hosting a variety of avant-garde performances and festivals, including the Sydney Writers' Festival *(see p54)*. There are a number of venues within the space, many of which still retain original features from the site's former life as a railway goods yard. The weekly farmers' market held from 8am to 1pm every Saturday is one of Sydney's best.

⑦ Jubilee, Bicentennial and Federal Parks
MAP B4

These three contiguous parks overlooking Rozelle Bay offer superb views of the city and the working harbour. A pathway follows the north shoreline from Rozelle to Blackwattle Bay. To the south is the old railway viaduct which threads its way past the historic grandstand in Jubilee Park to the restored Tramsheds complex. The stunning view from the small Pope Paul VI Reserve looks across Blackwattle Bay to the Anzac and Sydney Harbour bridges.

⑧ Glebe Markets
MAP K6

Every Saturday from 10am to 4pm, the grounds of Glebe Public School are used by market stalls selling new and second-hand clothes, records and bric-a-brac. A great source for flared trousers, leather jackets and sunglasses, Glebe Markets always offers unusual finds.

Stalls at the Carriageworks farmers' market

Sze Yup Buddhist Chinese Temple

9 Sze Yup Buddhist Chinese Temple

MAP B4 ■ Edward St ■ Open 9am–5pm daily

Sydney saw its first influx of Chinese immigrants soon after the discovery of gold in the region in the 1850s. The city's resultant Chinese community, the largest in Australia, built this temple on the site of a former market garden in 1898. It is named after a district in the Chinese province of Kwongtung. The traditional red and green temple was restored in 1978 and the archway added in 1982. The bones of the deceased were once kept here before being sent back to China for burial. Visitors are welcome, but do remember that this is an active place of worship and not a tourist attraction – dress respectfully and get permission before taking any photographs.

10 White Rabbit Gallery

MAP D5 ■ 30 Balfour St, Chippendale ■ 8399 2867 ■ www. whiterabbitcollection.org

This free showcase of modern Chinese art was established by Judith Neilson, one of Australia's richest women, after she travelled to China in the late 1990s. The collection includes more than 2,000 works by over 700 artists, and the gallery also houses a teahouse.

A WALK FROM NEWTOWN TO GLEBE

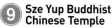

MORNING

Start your day in classic Newtown style with a strong coffee at **Black Star Pastry** *(325 King Street)*. Then follow Australia Street to Lennox Street and turn right. At the end is **St Stephen's Church**, designed by Edmund Blacket *(see p90)*. Beside the church is the entrance to the historic, peaceful **Camperdown Cemetery**. Soak in the Gothic atmosphere before heading back to hectic King Street. Check out the bookshops, cafés and funky clothing stores that run almost as far as Little Queen Street. Turn left, cross over Carillon Avenue and enter the manicured grounds of the **University of Sydney**. Turn right into Physics Lane, left into Fisher Road, and right into Manning Road, reaching the archway that leads through to the Main Quadrangle. Pass beneath the Gothic Revival clock tower and wander down University Avenue to the open space of **Victoria Park**. For lunch, head to trendy Glebe Point Road to vegetarian restaurant **Badde Manors**.

AFTERNOON

Follow Glebe Point Road to Pendrill Street, turn left and walk downhill to the **Sze Yup Buddhist Chinese Temple**. Turn right into Edward Street, left into Eglinton Lane, and right again into Edward Lane to reach **Jubilee Park**. Get a refreshment at Gelato Messina in the historic Tramsheds and stroll through the park to **Pope Paul VI Reserve**. When done, catch the Light Rail at the Jubilee Park stop to head back to Newtown.

See map on p114

Funky Shops

Exterior of Dangerfield

and obscure titles, and holds weekly events such as book launches and poetry readings.

5 Repressed Records
MAP B6 ▪ 413 King St, Newtown ▪ www.repressedrecords.com

This is the place to get the best imported, new and second-hand vinyl you're unlikely to find anywhere else.

6 Monster Threads
MAP B5 ▪ 251 King St, Newtown ▪ www.monsterthreads.co.au

Here, young illustrators turn everyday items of clothing, bags, homewares and accessories into masterpieces with creative graphic designs.

7 The Social Outfit
MAP C5 ▪ 188 King St, Newtown ▪ 9550 3691 ▪ www.thesocialoutfit.org

This sustainable fashion label has clothes made with donated fabrics. It provides employment and training to refugees and migrant communities.

8 Blue Dog Posters
MAP B5 ▪ 311 King St, Newtown ▪ 1300 781 0222 ▪ www.bluedogposters.com.au

A haven for pop culture aficionados, stocking the quirky, nerdy and unusual, including posters, art, frames and T-shirts, as well as a wide range of gifts.

9 Root'd
MAP K6 ▪ 62 Glebe Point Rd, Glebe ▪ www.rootd.com.au

Quirky and beautiful collections of plants, homewares, candles, gifts, ceramics, accessories and jewellery crafted by local creators.

10 Mineralism
MAP K6 ▪ 31 Glebe Point Rd, Glebe ▪ 9571 9179 ▪ www.mineralism.com.au

Expect crystals, cauldrons, incense, tarot books, meditation aids and large varieties of mineral specimens, fossils and gemstone jewellery.

1 Dangerfield
MAP C5 ▪ 268–270 King St, Newtown ▪ www.shop.dangerfield.com.au

An alternative Australian fashion brand that gives the latest street-wear styles a vintage feel.

2 U Turn
MAP C5 ▪ 305 King St, Newtown ▪ 9557 4724 ▪ www.uturn.com.au

A treasure trove of amazing and affordable vintage and second-hand clothing and accessories.

3 Dragstar
MAP B6 ▪ 535a King St, Newtown ▪ www.dragstar.com.au

Find new clothes in the style of traditional favourites, including T-shirt dresses, minis, shorts and tank tops.

4 Gleebooks
MAP K6 ▪ 49 Glebe Point Rd, Glebe ▪ www.gleebooks.com.au

This much-loved store is crammed with books, including academic

Restaurants

PRICE CATEGORIES
For a two-course meal for one with a drink (or equivalent meal), plus taxes and extra charges.

$ under $50 $$ $51–120 $$$ over $121

1 Tom-Tum Tum-Gang
MAP J5 ▪ 249 Glebe Point Rd, Glebe ▪ 8065 0859 ▪ Open 11am–9pm daily ▪ $
You'll spot this popular, no-frills Thai restaurant by the queue of locals awaiting their turn outside. Payment is in cash only.

2 Small Talk Coffee
MAP J5 ▪ 13/131–145 Glebe Point Rd, Glebe ▪ Open 8am–3pm daily ▪ www.smalltalkcoffee.com ▪ $
A little café with a small selection of tasty handrolled bagels, focaccia and pastries.

3 Sappho Cafe
MAP K6 ▪ 51 Glebe Point Rd, Glebe ▪ Open 10am–5pm Sun–Tue, 10am–10pm Wed–Sat ▪ www.sapphobooks.com.au ▪ $
After you've picked a book from the wonderful selection in-store, have a coffee and a light meal. Enjoy cocktails and live music most nights.

4 Faheem Fast Food
MAP B6 ▪ 194–196 King St, Newtown ▪ 9550 4850 ▪ Open 5pm–midnight daily ▪ $
This is an Indian and Pakistani food institution. Although the decor is basic, the classic curries and tandoori chicken make up for it. Only cash payment is accepted.

5 Italian Bowl
MAP B5 ▪ 255 King St, Newtown ▪ Open noon–10pm daily (to 11pm Fri & Sat) ▪ www.theitalianbowl.com.au ▪ $
This popular restaurant has all the familiar favourites: pastas, risotto and a wide range of chicken and veal dishes. It can be a bit noisy here.

6 Gigi Pizzeria
MAP B6 ▪ 379 King St, Newtown ▪ Open daily D ▪ www.gigipizzeria.com.au ▪ $
One of the city's finest Neapolitan-style pizzerias – the food is entirely plant-based.

7 Golden Lotus Vegan
MAP B6 ▪ 341–343 King St, Newtown ▪ Open daily L & D ▪ www.goldenlotus-vegan.com ▪ $
Vietnamese vegan cuisine, with a touch of Malaysian and Thai.

8 Two Chaps
MAP A6 ▪ 122 Chapel St, Marrickville ▪ Open 7:30am–3pm daily, Thu–Sat D ▪ www.twochaps.com.au ▪ $
Here, you can enjoy wholesome, rustic café fare by day and superb handmade pasta by night.

9 Sixpenny
MAP B5 ▪ 83 Percival Rd ▪ 9572 6666 ▪ Open Wed–Sat D, Sat & Sun L ▪ www.sixpenny.com.au ▪ $$$
Book a multi-course meal that subtly nods to Australia's colonial history. Expect the likes of kangaroo tartare.

10 Spice Alley
MAP L6 ▪ Kensington St, Chippendale ▪ Open 11am–9:30pm daily ▪ www.spicealley.com.au ▪ $
This is the go-to place for a wide range of delicious Asian street food.

Diners at Spice Alley

See map on p114 ←

TOP **10** Balmain and Pyrmont

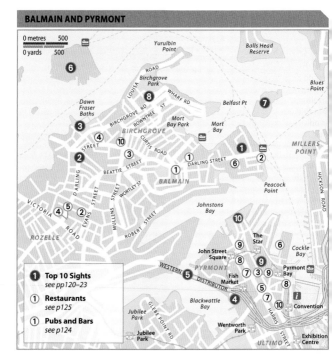

Sydney fish market sign

William Balmain, a surgeon on the First Fleet, was granted 223 ha (550 acres) west of the city in 1800, perhaps in gratitude for having tended to Governor Phillip after he was speared in 1790. The area was subdivided in the mid-1800s, and grand harbourside residences were erected alongside working-class stone and timber cottages and a multitude of pubs that catered to the employees of the local timber, mining and maritime industries. By the 1960s, Balmain had become a haven for writers, artists and actors, a reputation it still retains today. Pyrmont was originally the city's industrial heart, with shipbuilding and ironworks on the waterfront, two power stations, wool stores and sandstone quarries used for the construction of great 19th-century public buildings including the Sydney Town Hall and the University of Sydney. Following industrial decline in the second half of the 20th century, abandoned sites were gentrified, with the area now a hip hub for tech and media companies, with plenty of cafés and bars.

BALMAIN AND PYRMONT

0 metres 500
0 yards 500

Yurulbin Point
Balls Head Reserve
Blues Point
Birchgrove Park
Dawn Fraser Baths
Belfast Pt
Birchgrove
Mort Bay Park
Mort Bay
MILLERS POINT
Darling Street
BALMAIN
Peacock Point
Johnstons Bay
ROZELLE
The Star
Cockle Bay
John Street Square
Pyrmont Bay
PYRMONT
Fish Market
Convention
Blackwattle Bay
Jubilee Park
Wentworth Park
Exhibition Centre
ULTIMO

- **1** Top 10 Sights *see pp120–23*
- **1** Restaurants *see p125*
- **1** Pubs and Bars *see p124*

Colourful painted workshops in Mort Bay, Balmain

1 Balmain East
MAP C3

At the eastern end of the Balmain peninsula is the Darling Street Wharf, overlooked by manicured Thornton Park. A sign tracing the route of the Balmain History Trail can be found near the bus stop. On Darling Street, check out the former Dolphin Hotel and the Waterman's Cottage. To the south, Peacock Point offers great views over Millers Point, Darling Harbour and the Anzac Bridge.

2 Darling Street
MAP B3

Darling Street runs from the wharf in Balmain East to Victoria Road in Rozelle. It's a steady uphill climb from the wharf until you reach the friendly London Hotel, just before a large roundabout. En route you pass the childhood home of former New South Wales premier Neville Wran, No 117, and the 1854 Watch House at No 179, the oldest in Sydney. Find Gladstone Park past the roundabout, and St Andrew's across the road, which hosts the Balmain Markets every Saturday. From here on it's boutiques, cafés, bookshops and salons all the way to the Victorian courthouse, town hall, fire station and library (see p88).

3 Elkington Park
MAP B2 ■ Dawn Fraser Baths, Fitzroy Ave, Balmain ■ www.innerwest.nsw.gov.au

A lovely reserve on White Horse Point, overlooking Cockatoo Island,

it is best known for the Dawn Fraser Baths (see p57), one of Sydney's oldest municipal pools, built in the 1880s. Dawn Fraser is a local legend, as much loved for her candid take on life and wild streak as she is for having dominated the pool at the 1956, 1960 and 1964 Olympic Games. Including an outdoor saltwater tidal pool, the baths are open from October to April.

4 Sydney Fish Market
MAP K4 ■ Cnr Pyrmont Bridge Rd & Bank St, Pyrmont ■ Open 7am–4pm daily ■ www.sydneyfishmarket.com.au

This is the largest market of its kind in the southern hemisphere. The complex in Pyrmont is home to the fishing fleet, wholesale and retail fish markets, delicatessens, oyster, sushi and sashimi bars, cafés, restaurants, a bottle shop and a bakery. You can sit down and enjoy a seafood meal indoors or buy takeaway food and head to the picnic tables outside.

Shoppers at Sydney Fish Market

The spectacular eight-lane, cable-stayed Anzac bridge

5 Anzac Bridge
MAP J4

This stunning bridge was named in honour of Australia's World War I soldiers: Anzac stands for Australian and New Zealand Army Corps. It spans narrow Johnstons Bay and links Pyrmont with Rozelle and Balmain. Opened in 1995, this is the longest cable-stayed span bridge in Australia, and possibly its finest.

6 Cockatoo Island
MAP B2

Since European settlement, the largest of Sydney Harbour's islands has been used variously as a convict prison, granary, girls' reformatory, shipyard and docks. Sutherland Dock was completed in 1890 and the island became a major centre of the Australian shipbuilding industry. It also served as the naval dockyard for the Royal Australian Navy throughout World War I. The dockyards closed down in 1992 and the Sydney Harbour Federation Trust opened the island to the public. The trust runs activities, a campground, events and tours on the island (see p81).

7 Goat Island
MAP C2

Northeast of Balmain, Goat Island was one of Bennelong's (see p13) favourite picnic spots. In the 1830s the island was used as a gunpowder magazine and convict barracks. One prisoner, Charles "Bony" Anderson, tried numerous times to escape the barracks, receiving 1,200 lashes for his troubles. He was chained to a sandstone "couch" for two years as further punishment. The island later became a base for the Water Police and Fire Brigade, and in 1925 shipyards were built on its western side. In the 1990s it was the film set for the TV series *Water Rats*. Offering fabulous views of Sydney Harbour, the island is managed by the National Parks and Wildlife Service (see p18).

8 Birchgrove
MAP B2

This historic suburb has several colonial-era homes, a small shopping village on Rowntree Street and

OUR DAWNIE

Balmain's working-class community included many unconventional characters, none more so than swimming champion Dawn Fraser. Born into a poor family in 1937, she became the first woman to swim the 100 m freestyle in less than one minute. However, she also gained notoriety at the 1964 Tokyo Olympics when, desiring a souvenir in addition to her gold medals, Fraser stole the Olympic flag and was arrested.

Balmain and Pyrmont

Birchgrove Park, the site of Australia's first Rugby League match in 1908. The northern tip of Birchgrove is known as Yurulbin Point, formerly called Long Nose Point, which, along with Manns Point, forms the mouth of the Parramatta River. Yurulbin Park has spectacular views of the Harbour Bridge, and an interpretation board near the ferry wharf provides interesting details on the area's Aboriginal heritage.

9 The Star
MAP K3 ■ 80 Pyrmont St, Pyrmont ■ 9777 9000 ■ www.star.com.au/sydney

A huge entertainment complex that incorporates retail outlets, nightclubs, Sydney's only casino, the Lyric theatre, and myriad dining options, from fine dining to casual grab-and-go. The Star hosts major musicals, theatrical productions and the Australian music industry's celebrity-studded annual awards night.

10 Pirrama Park
MAP K3 ■ Pirrama Rd, Pyrmont

Formerly a water police base, the City of Sydney council acquired the land in 2005 and transformed it into a lovely harbourside green space with beautiful views of the western side of the Sydney Harbour Bridge. There is a playground for children and a small café on-site for the grown-ups. The Stevedore Walk tribute is a nod to the area's history of dockworkers and wooden wharves, some of which have been restored and integrated into the foreshore path.

Lush Pirrama Park by the harbour

A STROLL IN BALMAIN

▶ MORNING

Catch a ferry from Circular Quay (see p22) to the quaint **Balmain East Wharf**. Enter **Illoura Reserve** and walk south beneath she-oaks and other native trees to Peacock Point for views across to Darling Harbour (see p34). Johnston Street has great views of the Anzac Bridge. Head back to Darling Street (see p121) and admire some of Balmain's finest residences. Turn into Killeen Street and wander down through **Ewenton Park**. Around the corner is grand **Hampton Villa** overlooking the docklands, home of Sir Henry Parkes. Back at Darling Street, get a drink at the pleasant **London Hotel** (see p124). Then, window-shop all the way to the **Town Hall**. Backtrack to **the Cottage** (see p124) for an elegant lunch in the pretty garden setting.

AFTERNOON

After lunch, continue back down Darling Street to Mort Street and turn left. At the end is **Mort Bay Park**, site of the former Mort's Dock shipyards, named for Thomas Mort, which is now open harbourside parkland. Follow the shoreline around to the steps leading up to Wharf Road via Ronald Street. This lovely street leads to Snails Bay and the historic **Birchgrove Park**. A path traces the shoreline to Louisa Road, which has some very expensive real estate. Turn right and head towards **Yurulbin Park** for some spectacular harbour views before catching the ferry back to Circular Quay.

See map on p120

Pubs and Bars

1 London Hotel
MAP C3 ■ 234 Darling St, Balmain ■ 9555 1377 ■ www.the londonhotel.com.au

Established in 1870, this is one of the most atmospheric pubs in Sydney. Grab a tractor seat on the balcony, sip the west Australian wheat bear and enjoy Harbour Bridge views.

2 Welcome Hotel
MAP B3 ■ 91 Evans St, Rozelle ■ 9810 1323 ■ www.thewelcome hotel.com.au

The bistro at this Irish pub serves excellent food. Portions are generous and European flavours are infused with a Mediterranean influence.

3 The Cottage
MAP B3 ■ 342 Darling St, Balmain ■ www.thecottagebalmain. com.au

Take a seat in the front garden, leafy courtyard or behind the heritage façade and enjoy fine food and wine at this Balmain institution.

4 Riverview Hotel
MAP B2 ■ 29 Birchgrove Rd, Balmain ■ 9810 1151 ■ www. theriverviewhotel.com.au

This tiny local bar with its charming fin-de-siècle interiors and stylish decor is hidden in a backstreet but is certainly worth seeking out.

5 Quarryman's
MAP K4 ■ 214–16 Harris St, Pyrmont ■ 9660 0560 ■ www. quarrymans.com.au

A chilled watering hole with a relaxed vibe, an outdoor courtyard and more than 20 craft beers on tap.

6 East Village Hotel
MAP C3 ■ 82 Darling St, Balmain East ■ 9810 3333 ■ www. eastvillagebalmain.com.au

Balmain's second-oldest pub has excellent craft beer, couches to relax on and friendly owners who serve behind the bar.

Outside seating at Gallon

7 Gallon
MAP K3 ■ 117 Harris St, Pyrmont ■ 0402 799 557 ■ www. gallon.com.au

Step through the sandstone exterior into the most beautifully styled space in Pyrmont. This gorgeous wine bar has a delicious food menu in an intimate, unpretentious and welcoming environment.

8 The Terminus
MAP K3 ■ 61 Harris St, Pyrmont ■ 9692 0301 ■ www.terminuspyrmont. com

One of Sydney's oldest pubs, the Terminus was once home to a roll call of characters. Reopened in 2018 after being lovingly restored, it is a popular local watering hole.

9 Clementine
MAP K3 ■ 52 Harris St, Pyrmont ■ 8591 3660 ■ www.bistroclementine. com

An espresso bar and café by day, Clementine also serves wonderful cocktails. It is the wine that is the star of the show here, though.

10 Mister Percy
MAP L4 ■ 139 Murray St, Pyrmont ■ www.ovolohotels.com

This neighbourhood wine bar with a cool vibe is housed in an old woolstore and named for former wool classer and local personality, Percy Ewart.

Restaurants

PRICE CATEGORIES
For a two-course meal for one with a drink (or equivalent meal), plus taxes and extra charges.
....
$ under $50 $$ $51–120 $$$ over $121

1 Café d'Yvoire
MAP C3 ■ 189 Darling St, Balmain ■ 8386 2467 ■ $
A charming, pretty, light-filled, white-walled French patisserie and café framed by climbing green vines.

2 The Fenwick
MAP K1 ■ 2–8 Weston St, Balmain East ■ www.thefenwick. com.au ■ $$
Creative cooking and the best harbour views in Balmain on the foreshore.

Dish at The Fenwick

3 Quick Brown Fox
MAP K3 ■ 22 Union St, Pyrmont ■ www.quick brownfoxeatery.com.au ■ $
Visit this lively restaurant for its all-day menu of café favourites. Don't miss the waffles or breakfast congee.

4 Victoire
MAP B3 ■ 660 Darling St, Rozelle ■ 9818 5529 ■ $
Stop in for amazing cakes and pastries, crusty sourdough bread and excellent cheese.

5 Belle Fleur
MAP B3 ■ 658 Darling St, Rozelle ■ www.bellefleur.com.au ■ $
Handcrafted chocolates and truffles, many with unusual flavours such as wattleseed and lemon myrtle, all exquisitely decorated and boxed.

6 LuMi Bar and Dining
MAP L3 ■ 56 Pirrama Rd, Pyrmont ■ www.lumidining.com ■ $$$
Offering an intriguing spin on Italian food with an inventive Japanese twist

and set on one of Pyrmont's old repurposed wharves, this is one of Sydney's finest restaurants.

7 Social Brew
MAP K4 ■ 224 Harris St, Pyrmont ■ www.socialbrewcafe.com. au ■ $
A modern café in an industrial setting with a cool vibe in the heart of Pyrmont village.

8 The Little Snail
MAP L4 ■ 50 Murray St, Pyrmont ■ 9212 7512 ■ www. thelittlesnail.com.au ■ $$
This classic French bistro offers exceptional set lunch and dinner menus in a lovely modern space.

9 Sokyo
MAP K3 ■ The Star, 80 Pyrmont St, Pyrmont ■ www.star. com.au ■ $$$
Traditional Japanese cuisine is given an Australian twist at this restaurant. The dishes here are made using the finest local produce.

10 Contessa
MAP B3 ■ 371b Darling St, Balmain ■ www.contessabalmain. com.au ■ $
It's hard to miss the wonderful mural of "Contessa" that adorns an entire wall of this popular café. The expansive menu offers something for all.

Striking mural at Contessa

See map on p120

🔟 The North Shore

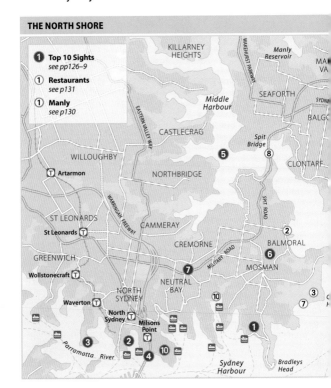

Sydney's affluent North Shore is an attractive blend of leafy suburbs north of the harbour, with waterways not far in any direction. Fine mansions sit on large blocks of land with beautifully kept gardens. Among the mansions of Sydney's well-to-do, you will find some glorious pockets of remnant bushland nestled around the harbour, with Balls Head Reserve offering some superb bushwalking trails far from the madding crowds. In addition, there are stunning ocean beaches, quiet harbourside bays, a sprinkling of smart waterside restaurants and plenty of options for those who love the great outdoors – walking, cycling, kayaking, surfing, diving, sailing and parasailing. Many of Sydney's perennially favourite tourist attractions are also located here: Luna Park, Nutcote, Taronga Zoo, Bradleys Head and Manly Beach. Take the Manly ferry from Circular Quay for the finest views of Sydney Harbour.

Luna Park sign

THE NORTH SHORE

1 **Top 10 Sights**
see pp126–9

1 **Restaurants**
see p131

1 **Manly**
see p130

1 Taronga Zoo

Just a short ferry ride from Circular Quay, Taronga Zoo offers some of Sydney's best harbour views alongside its extensive menagerie of more than 4,000 critters from Australia and beyond (see pp38–9). The zoo's work also includes an extensive conservation programme, centred around the preservation of endangered creatures.

2 Lavender Bay and Blues Point
MAP D2

East of Berry's Bay, this cove has great views of the Opera House framed by the Harbour Bridge. It was named after George Lavender, a boatswain who married the daughter of his neighbour Billy Blue (see p45). In 1817 Governor Macquarie granted Billy Blue 32 ha (80 acres) west of

Lavender Bay

Lavender Bay. In 1830, aged 82, Billy Blue established a ferry service from Dawes Point (see p16) to the headland that now bears his name.

3 Balls Head Reserve
MAP C2

On the headland east of Manns Point and the Parramatta River (see p123) lies this pleasant park, the site of Aboriginal rock art and bushwalking trails. It offers stunning views across the harbour to Goat Island (see p122) and Balmain (see p120). Barbecue facilities are available, and it's easily accessible from Waverton Railway Station. The park is cradled by the dormitory suburbs of Waverton and Wollstonecraft, the latter named after Edward Wollstonecraft, nephew of Mary Wollstonecraft, the author of *Rights of Women*.

4 Milsons Point
MAP D2

Nestled beneath the Harbour Bridge is a tiny suburb best known for its funfair, Luna Park (see p66), which is based on New York's Coney Island. Luna Park's famous laughing clown face set between two Art Deco towers has continuously overlooked the harbour since 1935, although it has been remodelled several times over the years. The park is built upon a former Sydney Harbour Bridge construction wharf and workshops and attracts more than one million visitors every year. Beside the park is the North Sydney Olympic Pool (see p57) which opened in 1936.

Dobroyd Head with North Head, South Head and Manly visible in the distance

5 Middle Harbour
MAP T3

The entrance to the northern arm of the harbour is marked by Middle Head and Dobroyd Head. North of Chinaman's Beach is the Spit Bridge, which can be raised, allowing boats to pass beneath. Castlecrag, northwest of the Spit Bridge, was home for a period to Walter Burley Griffin (1876–1937), the US architect who designed Australia's capital, Canberra. Much of Middle Harbour's shoreline is parkland; the calm waters are perfect for kayaking *(see p62)*. To the north of here is Garigal National Park *(see p58)*.

6 Mosman and Balmoral
MAP F1

Mosman Bay was named after Archibald Mosman, who established a whaling business nearby in 1830. The suburb is best known for Taronga Zoo *(see pp38–9)* and Bradleys Head *(see p58)*. Headland Park, which unites the former military lands at Chowder Bay, Georges Heights and Middle Head, offers harbourside walking tracks and several restaurants. Balmoral *(see p57)* has three beaches, including Chinamans Beach, a sheltered spot that's good for a relaxed swim or picnic.

7 Neutral Bay and Cremorne Point
MAP E2

Neutral Bay was named by Governor Phillip, who ordered that all foreign ships entering Sydney Harbour anchor here. Now this tranquil bay is home to the Royal Sydney Yacht Squadron, the Ensemble Theatre *(see p69)*, and the Sydney Flying Squadron. Children's author May Gibbs' residence, Nutcote *(see p54)*, is on the eastern slope. Further east is Cremorne Point, a long, narrow peninsula with a popular harbourside reserve.

8 Manly Peninsula
MAP U3 ■ Manly Visitor Information Centre: The Forecourt, Manly Wharf; 9976 1430

This peninsula was so named because Governor Phillip felt that the Aboriginal people he met here in 1788 were "manly" in appearance. In 1853, businessman Henry Smith purchased 121 ha (300 acres) on the formerly remote peninsula and set about creating a seaside pleasure resort. Today, Manly is a very popular

---

SURFING TAKES OFF

In the summer of 1914–15, local officials invited Hawaiian Olympic champion Duke Kahanamoku to attend swimming carnivals in Sydney. During his stay, "The Duke" made a board from sugar pine and gave surfing demonstrations at Manly and Freshwater beaches. This popularized the sport in Australia. His surfboard is shown at Freshwater surf club and a memorial stands in McKillop Park.

and lively destination. Home to great beaches, it also hosts October's Manly International Jazz Festival (see p83). Catch the enjoyable harbour ferry ride from Circular Quay and make a full day of it.

 Manly Scenic Walk
MAP U3

A 10-km (6-mile) walk, one of Sydney's very best, traces North Harbour's shoreline from Manly to the Spit Bridge. The walk passes by coastal heathlands, flat sandy beaches and subtropical rainforest. Highlights on the way include pretty Forty Baskets Beach, rugged Dobroyd Head, the 1911 Grotto Point Lighthouse, Clontarf Beach (see p56) and Aboriginal shell middens east of the Spit Bridge. The NPWS (see p18) offers a useful map of the route, available at the NPWS and Manly visitor information centres.

 Kirribilli
MAP D2

This smart waterfront suburb is best known for the two historic official residences that occupy its tip. The former residence of the Commander of the British Royal Navy, Admiralty House, constructed in 1843, is now the Sydney residence of the Governor General, Queen Elizabeth II's representative in Australia. Built in 1855, the neighbouring Gothic Revival–style Kirribilli House is the official Sydney residence of the Australian Prime Minister. Both these grand old houses are best admired from harbour ferries.

Admiralty House, Kirribilli

A BEACH WALK AROUND MANLY

MORNING

Pack a picnic lunch and catch the ferry from Circular Quay to Manly. Cross **The Esplanade** and follow **The Corso** down to **Manly Beach** (see p130). Head south and follow the path around to **Cabbage Tree Bay**, where you'll find the delightful **Fairy Bower** rock pool (see p57) and **Shelly Beach** (see p130), both of which are perfect for children. Then take some time out for your picnic and a swim.

AFTERNOON

Leave the beach via Bower Street and follow this around to College Street, past the million-dollar mansions overlooking Manly Beach. Turn right into Reddall Street, left into Addison Road, and left again into Darley Road. Head uphill and take a peek over the stone walls at the **Former St Patrick's Seminary** (see p130). Continue past the hospital and take the right fork leading into **Sydney Harbour National Park** (see p18). Pass beneath the sandstone arch and take Collins Beach Road on your right. This winds down through a lovely shaded gully to the **Police College**. A small path on your right leads to the secluded **Collins Beach** (see p130), one of Sydney's loveliest harbour beaches. A path at the end of the beach leads to Stuart Street, which takes you back to Manly. Finish your walk with a sun-downer at **Wharf Bar** (see p131), keeping your eyes peeled for fairy penguins, which come in to nest around the wharf between July and February.

See map on pp126–7

Manly

Pedestrians strolling along the Corso in Manly

① The Corso
MAP U3

This lively pedestrian avenue runs from the Esplanade to Manly Beach. The Manly Deli is a good place to stock up for a picnic lunch.

② Manly Cove
MAP U3

The ferry wharf houses a number of boutiques and cafés, a Visitor Information Centre, Manly Kayak Centre and the Manly Art Gallery and Museum. The latter hosts regular exhibitions and events, and also houses a shop selling works by local artists and designers.

③ Hotel Steyne
MAP U3 ■ 75 The Corso
 www.hotelsteyne.com.au

The most famous of the Corso's multi-level hotels, "the Steyne", opposite Manly Beach, also has the best views from its rooftop bar, Henry's.

④ 4 Pines Brewing Company
MAP U3 ■ 43–55 The Esplanade
■ www.4pinesbeer.com.au

Manly's original craft brewery serves hearty pub grub and beach views alongside its highly quaffable brews.

⑤ Manly Beach
MAP U3

Backed by a reserve lined with Norfolk Island pines and a busy esplanade, this ocean beach (see p56) is a Sydney favourite. There are rock baths at the northern end.

⑥ Cabbage Tree Bay
MAP U3

This bay has it all: shallow crystal-clear blue waters, dramatic wind-sculpted sandstone cliffs, the magical Fairy Bower rock pool (see p57) and protected Shelly Beach.

⑦ Former St Patrick's Seminary
MAP U3

This 1885 Catholic seminary was the setting for Thomas Keneally's novel *Three Cheers for the Paraclete* and featured in Baz Luhrmann's 2013 film *The Great Gatsby*.

⑧ North Head
MAP U3 ■ www.harbour trust.gov.au

This windswept highlight of the Sydney Harbour National Park (see p18) is home to diverse flora and fauna, and World War II relics. Take a self-guided walking tour.

⑨ Old Quarantine Station
MAP U3 ■ North Head, Sydney Harbour National Park ■ www. qstation.com.au

Until 1984, Sydney's infected arrivals were quarantined at this bulwark against infectious diseases. Try the ghost tours on offer here.

⑩ Collins Beach
MAP U3

The site where Governor Phillip was speared in 1790 is a peaceful spot nowadays. Steps lead to a secluded rock diving platform.

Restaurants

1 Wharf Bar
MAP U3 ▪ Manly Wharf, Manly ▪ 9977 1266 ▪ www.wharfbar.com.au ▪ $$

For a casual fish 'n' chips lunch by the sea, it's hard to beat this wharf-side restaurant and bar.

2 Bather's Bistro
MAP U3 ▪ 4 The Esplanade, Mosman ▪ 9969 5050 ▪ www.batherspavilion.com.au ▪ $$

Occupying a splendid Art Deco pavilion by Balmoral Beach, "the Bather's" dishes up superb modern Australian bistro fare with a price tag you'd expect for the setting.

3 Gunners Barracks Tea Room
MAP U3 ▪ Suakin Dr, Mosman ▪ www.gunnersbarracks.com.au ▪ $$

Enjoy one of Sydney's best high teas and superb harbour views from a veranda table at this historic building.

4 Chica Bonita
MAP U3 ▪ 9 The Corso, Manly ▪ 9976 5255 ▪ www.chicabonita.com.au ▪ $$

A charming casual restaurant that offers a small but tasty menu consisting of Mexican favourites. Wash them down with excellent margaritas. The atmosphere is lively and the staff attentive.

5 Busta
MAP U3 ▪ 10 Pittwater Rd, Manly ▪ 8966 9917 ▪ www.busta.com.au ▪ $$

This retro-glam modern Italian restaurant features a short, accessible menu with surprising combinations – think broccolini with pancetta.

6 Queen Chow
MAP U3 ▪ 43–45 East Esplanade, Manly ▪ www.merivale.com ▪ $$

Savour a huge dim sum platter or splurge on a lobster dinner at this Cantonese restaurant by the sea.

PRICE CATEGORIES

For a two-course meal for one with a drink (or equivalent meal), plus taxes and extra charges.

....

$ under $50 $$ $51–120 $$$ over $121

7 Ripples Chowder Bay
MAP U3 ▪ Deck C, Chowder Bay Rd, Mosman ▪ 9960 3000 ▪ www.rippleschowderbay.com.au ▪ $$

Enjoy harbour views and savour contemporary Italian-inspired food in a historic naval building.

8 Ormeggio at The Spit
MAP U3 ▪ D'Albora Marinas, Spit Rd, The Spit, Mosman ▪ 9969 4088 ▪ Closed Mon ▪ www.ormeggio.com.au ▪ $$$

It's worth booking to enjoy the sunset and the north Italian cuisine here, while overlooking Middle Harbour. The meat-free menu focuses on seafood and vegetable dishes.

9 Pilu at Freshwater
MAP U3 ▪ End of Moore Rd, Freshwater ▪ 9938 3331 ▪ Closed Mon ▪ www.pilu.com.au ▪ $$$

Sardinian-inspired cuisine includes oven-roasted suckling pig with a crispy skin.

Pilu at Freshwater

10 Mosman Rowers
MAP F1 ▪ 3 Centenary Ave, Mosman Bay ▪ 8006 8880 ▪ www.mosmanrowers.com.au ▪ $$

This club is a short walk from Mosman Bay wharf. The views from the balcony are spectacular.

See map on pp126–7

Pelican on the Hawkesbury River

TOP 10
Beyond Sydney

The region surrounding the city of Sydney offers a wealth of natural attractions, historic towns and villages, and outdoor activities. While many areas surrounding Sydney were impacted by the catastrophic summer bushfire season of 2019–2020 and some burnt bushland might be visible in places, the sights and townships listed are intact and remain well worth visiting. Some sights are located in Greater Sydney, others beyond Sydney's borders. All regions covered in this section are accessible by public transport, but hiring a car will give you greater flexibility. To the north of Sydney is Ku-ring-gai Chase National Park, the Hawkesbury River, the Central Coast and Hunter Valley. To the west are the famous Blue Mountains and historic Parramatta and Windsor, while to the south is the gorgeous Royal National Park and the Southern Highlands. Accommodation options range from luxury guesthouses to houseboats.

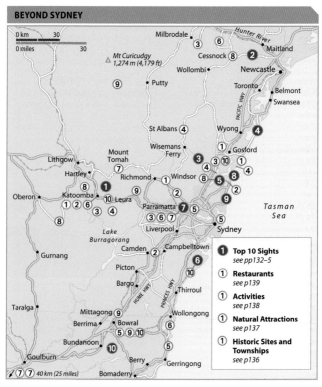

BEYOND SYDNEY

1 **Top 10 Sights**
see pp132–5

1 **Restaurants**
see p139

1 **Activities**
see p138

1 **Natural Attractions**
see p137

1 **Historic Sites and Townships**
see p136

Seven Sisters in the Blue Mountains

1 Blue Mountains

These World Heritage-listed mountains are named for their distinctive bluish haze, the result of evaporating eucalyptus oil. The rugged mountains offer numerous bushwalks and plenty of natural attractions, such as the Three Sisters, the Jenolan Caves and Wentworth Falls *(see p137)*. When the explorers Gregory Blaxland, William Lawson and WC Wentworth *(see p45)* traversed the 1,100-m (3,600-ft) range in 1813, they opened up the continent's grassland interior to white European settlement. The main township of Katoomba *(see p138)* is located about 107 km (56 miles) west of Sydney.

2 Hunter Valley

Grapes have been grown in this region since the 1830s. Now there are more than 60 vineyards and countless artisans producing condiments, cheese and other gourmet delicacies; some also contain restaurants or cafés. Most of the wineries surround Pokolbin and neighbouring Cessnock, which is the regional township closest to Sydney. Beautiful Hunter Valley is also a popular area for outdoor activities such as cycling, golf, horse riding and hot-air ballooning. Numerous tour operators in Sydney offer attractive day, overnight and weekend packages to the area.

3 Hawkesbury River
MAP U1

This broad river runs from Windsor *(see p136)* in the west to Broken Bay *(see p134)* in the east, passing massive sandstone escarpments, historic riverside towns, national parks, mangrove islands, fishing villages and holiday homes, as well as the spectacular Berowa Waters and Cowan Creek *(see p138)* coves and Pittwater *(see p134)*. Berowa Waters is home to the famous Berowa Waters Inn. Cowan Creek peters out near pretty Bobbin Head. Although parts of the river are popular with waterskiers, it's actually best enjoyed at a leisurely pace.

4 Central Coast
MAP U1

The coast from Broken Bay *(see p134)* to Newcastle offers glorious ocean beaches, national parks and several lakes and waterways. The main regional town is Gosford, at the head of Brisbane Water. This large waterway runs out to Broken Bay past Woy Woy and the townships of Hardy's Bay in Killcare, Pretty Beach and Wagstaffe. Behind Wagstaffe is Bouddi National Park *(see p137)*, which extends north to pleasant McMaster's Beach. Pearl Beach *(see p138)* and the fishing village of Patonga overlook Broken Bay.

Beautiful waters of the Central Coast

5 Ku-ring-gai Chase National Park

MAP T1 ■ Visitor Centre: via Bobbin Head; 9472 8949

Bounded by the Hawkesbury River to the north and Pittwater to the east, this gorgeous native bushland is a bushwalker's and kayaker's delight. There are numerous walking trails, picnic areas, secluded beaches and lookouts as well as hundreds of Aboriginal rock art sites. Stay at the Basin campsite, seek out a tucked-away restaurant overlooking the water at Cottage Point or anchor at the marinas at Akuna Bay and Bobbin Head. Cycling and horseriding are allowed in parts of the park. Flora and fauna highlights include banksias, waratahs, Sydney red gums, wallabies, flying foxes, pelicans, platypus, blue-tongued lizards, cockatoos and parrots. The information centre runs activities and provides maps and useful tips.

6 Royal National Park

MAP S6 ■ Sir Bertram Stevens Dr ■ Open 7:30am–8:30pm daily ■ www.nationalparks.nsw.gov.au

Proclaimed in 1879, this is Australia's oldest national park and the world's second oldest. The 15,074-ha (37,248-acre) park lies 32 km (19 miles) to the south of Sydney. Here you'll find subtropical rainforests, deep valleys, cycle and walking trails, rugged ocean beaches, sandstone clifftops, heathlands, mangroves and inland lagoons. There are several picnic spots and campgrounds, and if you are lucky you could spy a swamp wallaby, a satin bowerbird, a pied oystercatcher or the endangered tiger quoll. A tram from Loftus Station connects with the park's visitors' centre on Sundays and public holidays.

7 Parramatta

MAP S3 ■ St John's Cemetery: O'Connell St, Parramatta

Parramatta is part of Greater Sydney, just 20 km (13 miles) west of the city centre and easily accessible by the suburban train network. The fertile soil found here in the 1780s spared the fledgling colony from probable starvation and spawned Sydney's original satellite township. It was a rural retreat for Governor Phillip, who built a cottage here in 1790. Old Government House (see p136), which replaced Phillip's cottage in 1799, is one of Sydney's most historic sites. Other highlights include Experiment Farm Cottage, Elizabeth Farm, Hambledon Cottage (see p136) and Australia's oldest cemetery, St John's.

8 Pittwater and Broken Bay

MAP U1

Pittwater is a long, slender waterway running from Newport to Palm Beach (see p56), Ku-ring-gai Chase National Park and Broken Bay. Private wharves, exclusive houses and public marinas populate its eastern shoreline. Housing on the western coastline thins out as you head north, until you reach Ku-ring-gai Chase National Park, north of isolated Towlers Bay and exclusive Scotland Island. Pittwater's sheltered waters have long been a favourite haunt with yacht sailors. Broken Bay is a beautiful, wide and sometimes wild expanse of water dominated by Lion Island, an uninhabited rocky outcrop covered in vegetation.

Lion Island in Broken Bay

Lighthouse overlooking Palm Beach

⑨ Northern Beaches
MAP U1–3

This beautiful stretch of stunning ocean beaches runs from Manly to Barrenjoey Head. Palm Beach *(see p56)* is a picturesque haven for Sydney millionaires, as well as being the outdoor location for the long-running television soap opera *Home and Away*. The Barrenjoey Lighthouse overlooks Broken Bay, the Central Coast and the Hawkesbury River *(see p133)*. Behind Palm Beach lies the lovely waterway of Pittwater.

⑩ Southern Highlands

The coastal hinterland and the city of Wollongong, a couple of hours' drive south of Sydney, is a popular weekend getaway destination. With no shortage of antiques and crafts shops, galleries, B&Bs, English-style pubs, ivy-clad Georgian buildings and cottage gardens, this region is reminiscent of the English countryside. The beautiful town of Bowral *(p136)* is known for its gardens and as the home of Australia's greatest cricketer, Don Bradman. It traditionally served as a popular summer retreat for Sydney's gentry. Other must-see attractions in this area include the historic townships of Berrima, Berry and Kangaroo Valley. The movie *Babe* was filmed in the nearby village of Robertson.

A SCENIC DRIVE BY THE HAWKESBURY RIVER

▶ **MORNING**

Head north across the **Harbour Bridge** and take the M1, M2 and M7 to the **Old Windsor Road** exit *(see p136)*. After a pit stop at the 1815 **Macquarie Arms Hotel** on George Street, backtrack to Pitt Town Road and follow this northwards. It becomes Cattai Road and then the Wisemans Ferry Road, passing through farmland and bush before dropping down to **Wisemans Ferry** on the Hawkesbury River *(see p133)*. Take the southern ferry across the Hawkesbury and follow the incredibly scenic road that tracks the Macdonald River as far as St Albans *(see p136)*, where you can enjoy lunch at the **Settlers Arms Inn**, founded in 1848.

AFTERNOON

Head back towards Wisemans Ferry along the other side of the Macdonald River until it meets the Hawkesbury River. Follow the river beneath its sandstone escarpments and through the isolated riverside townships of **Gunderman** and **Spencer** before climbing up through the forest to **Central Mangrove**. Drop down to **Calga** via Peats Ridge and take the Old Pacific Highway south to the Hawkesbury again. Cross the river and take the turnoff to the small fishing and boating township of **Brooklyn**. Enjoy a refreshment at the waterfront King Tide Café or take a 15-minute ferry trip across to Dangar Island's idyllic **Dangar Island Depot** for homemade bread and jam and coffee overlooking the water.

See map on p132

Historic Sites and Townships

① Windsor
This town's Colonial buildings include one of Australia's oldest pubs, the 1815 Macquarie Arms Hotel, as well as the 1823 St Mathew's Anglican Church and Rectory, designed by Francis Greenway (see p29).

② Rouse Hill House and Farm
Guntawong Rd, Rouse Hill ■ 9627 6777 ■ Open 10:30am–3:30pm Sat & Sun (guided tours only) ■ Adm
This 1813 Sydney Living Museums property features a Georgian residence and gardens. The furniture dates from the 1830s to the 1960s. Booking ahead is advisable.

③ Experiment Farm Cottage
MAP S4 ■ 9 Ruse St, Harris Park ■ 9635 8149 ■ Open 10:30am–3:30pm 1st and 3rd weekend each month ■ Adm ■ www.nationaltrust.org.au
Emancipated convicts James and Elizabeth Ruse established Australia's first self-sufficient farm in 1789. In the colony's first land grant, Governer Phillip gave them a further 12 ha (30 acres) for their efforts.

④ St Albans
Settlers Arms Inn: 1 Wharf St; 4568 2111; www.settlersarms.com.au
The highlight of this quaint historical village is the charming Settlers Arms Inn, built by convict labour between 1836 and 1848.

⑤ Elizabeth Farm
MAP S4 ■ 70 Alice St, Rosehill ■ 9635 9488 ■ Open 10am–4pm Fri & Sat ■ Adm ■ www.sydneyliving museums.com.au
This 1793 estate was once a social, political and cultural centre. The farm's cottage is the oldest surviving building in Australia.

⑥ Hambledon Cottage
MAP S3 ■ 63 Hassall St, Parramatta ■ 9635 6924 ■ Open 11am–4pm Sat & Sun ■ Adm ■ www.hambledoncottagemuseum.org.au
Close by Elizabeth Farm, this pretty cottage was named after a village in Hampshire, England.

⑦ Old Government House
MAP S3 ■ Parramatta Park, Parramatta ■ www.nationaltrust.org.au
Overlooking the Parramatta River, this plastered brick residence is the country's oldest public building. It is set on 105 ha (260 acres) of parkland.

⑧ Rock Art in Ku-ring-gai Chase National Park
The area from Broken Bay to Sydney Harbour was once inhabited by the Guringai people. More than 800 sites here (see p134) record their culture.

⑨ Norman Lindsay Gallery
14 Norman Lindsay Crescent, Faulconbridge ■ www.nationaltrust.org.au
Artist and writer Norman Lindsay (1879–1969) occupied this property from 1912 until his death.

⑩ Bowral
Bradman Museum: St Jude St, Bowral; www.bradman.com.au
The Southern Highlands' main town was established in the 1860s and has an arty, old-world feel. It is probably best known as the former home of the famous cricketer Sir Donald Bradman (see p63).

Settlers Arms Inn, St Albans

Natural Attractions

Bouddi National Park terrain

1 Bouddi National Park
www.nationalparks.nsw.gov.au
With clifftop walks overlooking the ocean and Broken Bay, secluded beaches, heathlands and banksia forests, this tiny coastal park is a gem. It extends from Box Head to McMaster's Beach on the Central Coast and offers good bushwalking trails and camping facilities.

2 Australian Botanic Garden Mount Annan

Mt Annan Dr, Mt Annan ■ 4634 7900 ■ Open 8am–5pm daily (to 7pm in summer) ■ Adm ■ www.australian botanicgarden.com.au
On display at this amazing Botanic Garden is 404 ha (1,000 acres) of colourful and bizarre Australian plant life.

3 Three Sisters
The most popular landmark of the Blue Mountains (see p133) is this spectacular rock formation, which derives its name from an Aboriginal Dreamtime legend.

4 Wentworth Falls
These impressive 300-m (1,082-ft) falls mark the start of some of the Blue Mountains' most challenging walking trails to Jamison Valley.

5 Kiama Blowhole
This 25-m (82-ft) blowhole, in the laid-back seaside town of Kiama, originates in a natural fault in the cliffs. It erupts whenever a wave hits with enough force, which can be every few minutes. Water might be thrown as high as 60 m (200 ft).

6 Illawarra Coast
A sandstone escarpment that traces the coastline south of Royal National Park and north of Wollongong.

7 Blue Mountains Botanic Gardens Mount Tomah
Bells Line of Rd, Mt Tomah ■ Open 9am–5pm daily ■ www.blue mountainsbotanicgarden.com.au
Covering 28 ha (60 acres), these alpine gardens are located on a summit of the Blue Mountains. The rich basalt soil lies 1,000 m (3,281 ft) above sea level. Along with stunning views, the gardens feature an excellent collection of cool-climate plants. Follow the Botanists' Way trail to get here.

8 Jenolan Caves
1300 76 33 11 ■ Tours daily ■ Adm ■ www.jenolancaves.org.au
More than 300 chambers make up this striking complex of vast underground limestone caves, which lies southwest of Katoomba (see p138) in the Blue Mountains (see p133).

9 Wollemi National Park
This scenic park is the largest wilderness area in NSW at 492,976 ha (1.2 million acres). The rugged terrain is composed of a maze of canyons and gorges that traverse rainforested mountains. Highlights include riverside beaches, rafting and camping.

10 Brisbane Water National Park
MAP U1
Aboriginal rock art and spring wildflowers are the highlights of this 12,000-ha (39,640-acre) park overlooking the Hawkesbury River and Broken Bay. There are great views from the path leading from Pearl Beach to tiny Patonga, accessible by ferry from Palm Beach (see p56).

See map on p132 ←

Activities

Australian Reptile Park entrance

① Australian Reptile Park
Pacific Highway, Somersby (next to Gosford exit on F3) ▪ 4340 1022 ▪ Open 9am–5pm daily ▪ Adm ▪ www.reptilepark.com.au

Crocodiles, alligators, snakes, spiders and friendly kangaroos are all here.

② Sail Pittwater and Cowan Creek
MAP U1 ▪ Hardy's Bay Yacht Charters: Cnr Killcare Rd & Araluen Dr; 0412 260 085; www.hardysbayyacht charters.com.au

Hire a yacht and pack a picnic lunch to explore these isolated coves.

③ Swim at Pearl Beach
MAP U1

This National Trust hamlet is cradled by Brisbane Water National Park (see p137). The calm waters and rock pool are absolutely magical.

④ Riverboat Postman
Departs Brooklyn public wharf 10am Mon–Fri (bookings essential) ▪ www. riverboatpostman.vpweb.com.au

Join the local postman on a three-hour cruise delivering mail to those living on the Hawkesbury River.

⑤ Seaplane to Lunch
For a romantic lunch, take a seaplane from Rose Bay (see p109) to the Cottage Point Inn on Cowan Creek, or enjoy a picnic at Pittwater.

⑥ Visit Katoomba
Katoomba is the site of Echo Point, which offers superb views of the iconic Three Sisters, in the Blue Mountains. Take a bushwalk around the clifftop paths or head down the Giant Stairway, across Jamison Valley and back up on the Scenic Railway.

⑦ Overnight Trip to Canberra
Highlights of Australia's capital (a three-hour drive south from Sydney) include the Parliament Houses, the National Gallery, the War Memorial, the National Library, Lake Burley Griffin and Black Mountain.

⑧ Hot-Air Ballooning over Hunter Valley
www.balloonaloft.com/locations/ hunter-valley

Get up early for a bird's-eye view of sunrise with a hot-air balloon ride over the picturesque Hunter Valley then tuck into a gourmet Champagne breakfast at a winery back on the ground.

Hot-air balloon

⑨ Southern Highlands
A quaint English-village feel permeates towns such as Bowral and Mittagong. Their main streets are lined with teahouses and antique shops.

⑩ Premier's Walk
This 26-km (16-mile) route through the Royal National Park (see p134) offers ocean views and seasonal glimpses of migrating whales. You can walk a section or go for the whole two-day stretch.

Restaurants

1 Darley's
Lilianfels Resort & Spa, Katoomba ▪ Open Tue–Sat D ▪ www.darleysrestaurant.com.au ▪ $$$

Flawless Australian cuisine is served in a listed homestead with original fireplaces and breathtaking views.

2 Avalon
18 Katoomba St, Katoomba ▪ 4782 5532 ▪ Open Mon, Wed–Fri D, Sat & Sun L & D ▪ www.avalonkatoomba.com.au ▪ $$

Located inside the former 1930s Savoy Picture Theatre, with sweeping views over the Jamison Valley. The hearty dishes incorporate European, Australian and Asian influences.

3 Margan Restaurant
1238 Milbrodale Rd, Broke 2330 ▪ 6579 1372 ▪ Open Fri & Sat L & D, Sun L ▪ www.margan.com.au ▪ $$$

Enjoy beautifully prepared food, much of it grown on the estate surrounding this restaurant, in an elegant dining room overlooking vineyards.

4 Killcare Beach Kiosk
81 Beach Dr, Killcare ▪ 4360 1330 ▪ Open daily L ▪ www.killcarebeachkiosk.com ▪ $

Beachside dining on the ground floor of Central Coast's Killcare Surf Life Saving Club. Order food, drinks and coffee to eat in or take away.

5 Leila's at the Grand
Grand Arcade, 295–9 Bong Bong St, Bowral ▪ 4862 2126 ▪ Open Tue–Sun brunch & D ▪ www.leilasatthegrand.com.au ▪ $$

At this spot in the Southern Highlands, find hearty portions of Lebanese cuisine made with a modern twist.

6 Muse Kitchen
Hungerford Hill Winery, Hermitage & Deasys Rd, Pokolbin ▪ 4998 7899 ▪ www.musekitchen.com.au ▪ $$$

An award-winning Hunter Valley cellar-door restaurant serving contemporary Australian cuisine.

7 Temporada
15 Moore St, Canberra ▪ Open 7:30am–late Mon–Fri, 5pm–late Sat ▪ www.temporada.com.au ▪ $$

A stylish but casual, contemporary restaurant and bar with an inviting wood-panelled interior.

8 The Megalong Valley Tearooms
824 Megalong Valley Rd, Megalong Valley ▪ 4787 9181 ▪ $

Nestled beneath the upper Blue Mountains escarpment, this delightful tearoom serves breakfast and lunch.

9 Coffee Culture
Shop 6, Empire Cinema Complex, 327 Bong Bong St, Bowral ▪ 4862 2400 ▪ $

It's a local secret that the best coffee in the Southern Highlands comes from this aromatic shop.

10 Leura Garage
84 Railway Parade, Leura ▪ www.leuragarage.com.au ▪ $$

Formerly a mechanic's garage, the bar was made from a converted car hoist. Dishes here use local produce.

The interior of Leura Garage

See map on p132

Streetsmart

**Surfboards stacked outside
a shop at Manly Beach**

Getting Around

Arriving by Air

Sydney's only international airport is **Kingsford Smith International Airport**, which lies 9 km (5.6 miles) south of the city centre. All domestic flights also arrive and depart from here. The journey between the international (T1) and domestic terminals (T2 and T3) takes about ten minutes. To transit between terminals, you can use the airport's free T-bus or take the airport link train (two minutes).

Airport Link Trains provide a fast and easy way to get into the city, particularly during peak hours when traffic is heavy. The trip generally takes around 13 minutes. The International Station is directly under the arrivals area in T1; to reach the Domestic Station, follow the signs from the arrivals hall to the station entrance located in the car park across the road.

Two government-owned bus routes service the airport. Though very inexpensive, these are only a good option if you are heading east to Mascot, Randwick, Kensington or Bondi Junction (400 route), or southwest to Rockdale or Burwood (420 route).

There are several private airport shuttle operators. The largest fleet is run by **Redy2Go**, which has booking desks at both T1 and T2.

There are also taxi ranks outside each terminal. A taxi from T1 to Sydney city centre costs about $50–75 depending on the time of day. There is a toll of $4.75 payable on all taxi rides taken from the airport. Taxi queues are longest on weekdays at 7–9am and 5–7pm.

Rideshare is legal in Sydney and there is a specified rideshare waiting area at both the international and domestic terminals. **Uber**, **DiDi** and **Ola** are the biggest operators.

Children under seven years must use a child restraint in rideshare or hire vehicles (those under six months of age must travel in a rear-facing one). **Bubs Taxi** and **Ladies Running Errands** offer airport transfers for families with children who require car seats.

Arriving by Train

All interstate and regional trains terminate at Central Station. Sub-urban train services run from the lower level; buses to the eastern suburbs leave from Eddy Avenue, and those to the inner-west suburbs from nearby Railway Square. There is a taxi rank on the upper-level entrance.

Arriving by Coach

Many long-distance coach services terminate at the Sydney Coach Terminal in Eddy Avenue. Coach services operate along the east coast south to Melbourne, north to Brisbane and Cairns and west to Canberra. The main operators include **Greyhound** and **Murrays**.

Arriving by Sea

Sydney has two ports: the Overseas Passenger Terminal (OPT) at West Circular Quay and White Bay Cruise Terminal near Balmain. The OPT is a convenient place to arrive, as it is centrally located and close to many hotels. White Bay is a few minutes from the city centre, but taxis and shuttles are plentiful. **Captain Cook Cruises** offer a transfer service to King Street Wharf for some White Bay cruises.

Public Transport

Sydney has an extensive public transport system that includes metro, train, bus, ferry and light rail services. A single inte-grated ticketing system named Opal is in use for all of them, regardless of the operator. You can buy an Opal Card at the airport, all stations, newsagents and most convenience stores. The **Transport for NSW** web-site has timetables and maps for all services.

Bus

Services run frequently and are a good, fairly inexpensive way to get around. Route signs marked with an "L," "E" or "X" denote express or limited-stop services.

Train and Metro

Trains to most areas leave from the Town Hall, Wynyard and Central stations. Services run frequently from before 6am until after midnight. The City Circle line travels between Central and Circular Quay.

The rail network also includes the Metro North West Line, which runs between Tallawong and Chatswood.

Light Rail

Three light rail lines run between the city centre and the suburbs: L1 travels west from Central Station via Darling Harbour and the Fish Market to Dulwich Hill; L2 travels east from Circular Quay to Moore Park and Randwick Racecourse; and L3 runs from Circular Quay to Kensington and Kingsford.

Ferry

Both private and public ferry services operate on Sydney Harbour and west up the Parramatta River, offering great views of the city while travelling around. Public ferries are usually green and yellow.

Taxi

Taxis operate via several main ranks in the city and you can also flag them down in the street. There are also several ridesharing operators *(see p142)*. Taxi fares are regulated and cost more after 10pm. There is a variable set of tolls that must be paid for all harbour crossings.

Driving

Drivers with a valid overseas licence printed in English can drive in Australia for a maximum of three months. Driving in the Central Business District (CBD) can be challenging, as there are many one-way streets. Parking is also very expensive in the city centre.

To hire a car, a credit card and passport are required. Car hire companies, including **Avis**, **Budget**, **Europcar** and **Hertz**, have desks at the airport, but it's advisable to shop around.

When driving, you must always carry your licence. The use of seatbelts is compulsory, and it is forbidden to use a mobile phone while in control of a vehicle. You must maintain a blood alcohol level below 0.05 when you are behind the wheel. Fines for driving offences are doubled during holiday periods.

Cycling

There are several bike share schemes, including e-bikes. The **City of Sydney** website has details of the options available, as well as a useful cycling map for the city. Cyclists are required by law to wear a helmet and it is illegal to ride on the footpath.

Walking

Walking around Sydney is a great way to see the city. It is generally safe and individual districts are mostly small enough to explore on foot.

Practical Information

Passports and Visas

For entry requirements, including visas, consult your nearest Australian embassy or check the **Australian Department of Home Affairs** website. All visitors need a passport valid for longer than their intended stay and a visa to enter Australia. Only New Zealand passport holders can apply for a visa on arrival. The eVisitor visa (subclass 651) and Electronic Travel Authority (subclass 601) are free and allow multiple visits within a 12-month period with a maximum stay of three months each time. The visitor visa (subclass 600), which allows a stay of up to 12 months, starts at $370. Visa eligibility can vary by country of origin.

Government Advice

Now more than ever, it is important to consult both your government and the Australian government's advice before travelling. The **UK Foreign and Commonwealth Office**, the **US State Department** and the website of the **Australian Government** offer the latest information on security, health and local regulations.

Customs Information

Find information on the laws relating to goods and currency taken in or out of Australia on the **Australian Border Force** website. Note that some foods, plant material and animal products are not allowed into Australia. Prohibited items include fresh and packaged food, eggs, meat, plants, seeds, skins and feathers.

Travel Insurance

We recommend taking out a comprehensive insurance policy covering theft, loss of belongings, medical care, cancellations and delays, and to read the small print carefully.

Australia has reciprocal health care agreements with a number of countries. Visitors from the UK are entitled to free emergency treatment, and some subsidized health services, via Australia's **Medicare** system. Visitors from the US are not covered.

Health

Australia has a world-class health care system. Emergency medical care is free for visitors from countries with reciprocal health care agreements with Australia *(see above)*. Make sure your travel insurance covers ambulance fees, as they can be expensive.

Pharmacies can be found all over Sydney. In general they open seven days a week, particularly in shopping centres. It's advisable to carry your prescription if you require regular medication.

Take precautions against the strong Australian sun, as even overcast days can have a high UV rating. When swimming or sailing, keep in mind that water amplifies the intensity of UV rays.

Wear sturdy shoes and long trousers if you are walking in bushland, and check for ticks afterwards.

For information about COVID-19 vaccination requirements, consult government advice. A yellow fever certificate is required if you have come from, or visited, an infected country in the six days before your arrival in Australia.

Unless otherwise stated, tap water in Sydney is safe to drink.

Smoking, Alcohol and Drugs

Smoking is banned in almost all public spaces. Signs indicate designated smoking areas. Alcohol and tobacco products cannot be sold or supplied to those under the age of 18. Illegal drug use, possession and supply is not tolerated.

ID

Passports are required as ID at airports. Visits and tours to some government buildings require photo ID. Anyone who looks under 18 may be asked for ID as proof of age to enter licensed premises or to buy alcohol and cigarettes.

Personal Security

Sydney is a generally safe city, with a low crime rate. Pickpocketing is not a big problem, but it's always advisable to use your common sense, keep valuables in a safe place, and be alert to your surroundings. If you have anything stolen, report the crime as soon as possible at the nearest police station. Get a copy of the crime report in order to make a claim on your insurance. Contact your embassy or consulate immediately if your passport is stolen or in the event of a serious crime or accident.

Unless you are an experienced open-water swimmer, stick to beaches patrolled by lifeguards and always swim between the red-and-yellow flags.

Bushfires are part of life in Sydney's outer suburbs. "Total Fire Ban" days are often declared in summer. If you see a fire, avoid it; seek shelter immediately.

Ambulance, **police** and **fire** services can be called for free from any landline or mobile. For advice about bushfires, visit the **Fire and Rescue NSW** website.

Although same-sex marriage was only legalized in 2017, Sydney's local government began granting partnership benefits and relationship recognition to same-sex couples from 2005. Today, the city has one of the largest LGBTQ+ populations and pride festivals in Australia. If you do feel unsafe, the **Safe Space Alliance** pinpoints your nearest place of refuge.

First Nations peoples have faced historic prejudice and discrimination. Aboriginal peoples and Torres Strait Islanders weren't included in the country's census until 1967, and inequality persists today. The National Aboriginal Community Controlled Health Organisation (**NACCHO**) offers support and services for First Nations peoples.

Travellers with Specific Requirements

The **City of Sydney** website has detailed advice on the accessibility of the city's attractions and transport. The site also includes an accessibility map and a map of mobility parking. The **Travel Without Limits** website has reviews of accessible attractions and tours, while the government's **Public Toilet Map** website shows the location of public toilets and identifies accessible ones.

Much of Sydney's public transport network is accessible. Buses that have accessible entry and exit points and secure facilities for wheelchairs are clearly marked on the city bus timetable. Most ferry wharves in Sydney are also fully accessible, and travelling by ferry is a particularly good way of getting around the area beyond the city centre. There is a good supply of accessible accommodation across the city, but it can book up quickly during high season.

Theatres and concert halls offer accessible seating and options for visually and hearing impaired visitors, and major galleries run guided tactile and sensory tours. Check individual websites for details.

DIRECTORY

PASSPORTS AND VISAS

Australian Department of Home Affairs
w immi.homeaffairs.gov.au

GOVERNMENT ADVICE

Australian Government
w australia.gov.au

UK Foreign and Commonwealth Office
w gov.uk/foreign-travel-advice

US State Department
w travel.state.gov

CUSTOMS INFORMATION

Australian Border Force
w abf.gov.au

TRAVEL INSURANCE

Medicare
w servicesaustralia.gov.au

PERSONAL SECURITY

Ambulance, Police, Fire
c 000

Fire and Rescue NSW
w fire.nsw.gov.au

NACCHO
w naccho.org.au

Safe Space Alliance
w safespacealliance.com

TRAVELLERS WITH SPECIFIC REQUIREMENTS

City of Sydney
w cityofsydney.nsw.gov.au/lists-maps-inventories/accessibility-map-city-centre

Public Toilet Map
w toiletmap.gov.au

Travel Without Limits
w travelwithoutlimits.com.au

Time Zone

Sydney is on Australian Eastern Standard Time UTC +10. Eastern Daylight-Saving time begins when clocks go forward by one hour on the first Sunday in October and ends on the first Sunday in April.

Money

The currency in Australia is the Australian dollar, which is divided into 100 cents. Contactless payments are widely used in Sydney (up to a limit of $100), and almost all establishments accept major credit, debit and prepaid currency cards. Very few outlets insist on cash, but small stores may impose a surcharge for card payments under $10–15, so it is useful to carry some cash in small denominations. ATMs are widely available, though note that some can charge high fees.

There is no need to tip anywhere but the fanciest of restaurants, where you should add 10 per cent to the total bill.

Electrical Appliances

Voltage in Australia is 230V 50Hz. This is compatible with most European countries, but travellers from Japan, USA and Canada may need an electrical converter if their appliance does not have a dual voltage facility. Australian electric plugs have two flat pins that form a V-shape, while sometimes a third flat pin is present as well.

Mobile Phones and Wi-Fi

Free wi-fi is widely available, including in major shopping centres and even at Bondi and Manly beaches.

If you plan to use your phone often, you can buy a pay-as-you-go SIM card at the airport or a phone store, convenience store or supermarket, which can be used in any compatible phone.

Postal Services

Australia Post branch hours vary, but most post offices are open from 9am to 5pm Monday to Friday. The General Post Office (GPO) is open from 8:15am to 5:30pm Monday to Friday and 10am to 2pm Saturday. Stamps are also available from news agencies. They cost $1.10 within Australia and $2.50 for letters or cards being sent abroad.

Weather

Late spring (October–November) and early autumn (March–April) are the best times to visit Sydney. The days are warm and the evenings mild. Sydney's winters are cool to mild, but summer can be hot and humid with the occasional downpour. June and July can be great for savings, as while temperatures are lower the weather is often fine and sunny.

Opening Hours

Banks are open from 9:30/10am to 4/5pm Monday to Friday. Most shops are open daily 9am–5:30/6pm from Monday to Saturday, with some closing at 4pm on Sundays. Sydney City Westfield trades 9:30-7pm, Monday to Saturday. Late-night shopping on Thursdays sees shops open until 9pm. Museums and galleries are generally open 10am–5pm, with some offering late opening on one night per week. Times do vary though, so it is best to check before visiting.

Banks, post offices and most government agencies are closed on these public holidays: New Year's Day, Australia Day (26 January), Good Friday and Easter Monday, Anzac Day (25 April), Queen's Birthday (2nd Monday in June), Bank Holiday (1st Monday in August), Labour Day (1st Monday in October), Christmas Day and Boxing Day (25 and 26 December).

COVID-19 Increased rates of infection may result in temporary opening hours and/or closures. Always check ahead before visiting museums, attractions and hospitality venues.

Visitor Information

The main **Sydney Visitor Centre** is located in the Rocks; you can collect maps, guides and information for touring both Sydney and the rest of the country from here. There are also kiosks at Customs House, Kings Cross and Manly.

If you're planning to explore on foot, then it's worth downloading the

Sydney Culture Walks app, which features 18 themed city walks of varying lengths and degrees of difficulty. Walking tours are also offered twice a day by **I'm Free**; although these are completely free of charge, tips are expected.

Another good overview of the city is offered by **Big Bus Sydney**, the city's "hop-on, hop-off" tourist bus service. It operates two routes: one around the city centre and the other in the area around Bondi beach. Tickets are valid for either 24 or 48 hours. A similar hop-on, hop-off ferry service around the harbour is offered by **Captain Cook Cruises**.

For activities and attractions for families, the **Hello Sydney Kids** website is a great starting point, brimming with ideas for how to have fun with your children while visiting Sydney.

The **Visit Gay Australia** website provides plenty of information about accommodation and events for LGBTQ+ visitors, while the *Sydney Star Observer* is Australia's longest-established publication for LGBTQ+ people, carrying news and entertainment listings that are updated every month.

For an insider's take on the city, **Sydney Greeters** offers a free service that will match visitors to a local Sydneysider who will show you one of their favourite parts of the city. Tours last approximately three to four hours and require you to apply three weeks in advance for the best chance of a successful booking.

Local Customs

Dress and act respectfully in places of worship and sacred sites. When visiting sites that are sacred for First Nations peoples, read signage carefully, keep to dedicated paths and camping areas, and show respect for the local community and their beliefs. It's best to explore a site in the company of an Aboriginal guide.

Language

Australia has no official language, but English is the most widely spoken. Over 250 Aboriginal languages existed before European settlement, but now only around 100 survive.

Taxes and Refunds

A 10 per cent goods and services tax (GST) is applied to most items and included in the price displayed. If you spend $300 or more with a single store or business, you can claim back the GST paid through the **Tourist Refund Scheme**. To claim, you will need to submit your original tax invoices at an international airport's departure area, online or via a mobile app within 60 days of leaving Australia.

Accommodation

Accommodation in Sydney falls into the following categories: hotels rated between one and six stars; hostels with dormitories; B&Bs; apartments; and student residences, which offer cheap summer stays.

The Sydney tourist office provides a database of accommodation in all categories. Hotels can be booked through the tourism website, via an independent online booking portal, or directly with the hotel. Hostels, meanwhile, are not just for backpackers, as most offer comfortable double and twin rooms for modest prices.

Availability and rates vary hugely depending on the time of year. Book well in advance for travel at Christmas, New Year and Easter, and during festivals and school holidays.

DIRECTORY

POSTAL SERVICES

Sydney GPO
MAP M3 ■ 1 Martin Place
w auspost.com.au

VISITOR INFORMATION

Big Bus Sydney
w bigbustours.com/en/sydney

Captain Cook Cruises
w captaincook.com.au

Hello Sydney Kids
w hellosydneykids.com.au

I'm Free
w imfree.com.au/sydney

Sydney Greeters
w internationalgreeter.org/destinations/sydney

Sydney Visitor Centre
MAP M1 ■ 12–24 Playfair Street, the Rocks
w sydney.com

Visit Gay Australia
w visitgayaustralia.com.au

TAXES AND REFUNDS

Tourist Refund Scheme
w abf.gov.au

Places to Stay

PRICE CATEGORIES
For a standard, double room per night (with breakfast if included), taxes and extra charges.

$ under $175 $$ $175–350 $$$ over $350

Luxury Hotels

Four Seasons Sydney
MAP M2 ▪ 199 George St ▪ 9250 3100 ▪ www.four seasons.com ▪ $$$
The Four Seasons has harbour views from over half of its rooms, with corner rooms treated to a full panorama taking in the Opera House and Harbour Bridge.

Hilton Hotel Sydney
MAP M4 ▪ 488 George St ▪ 9266 2000 ▪ www. hiltonsydney.com.au ▪ $$$
Centrally located opposite the Queen Victoria Building, the Hilton has modern guest rooms with great workspaces, making it a top pick for business travellers.

The Langham
MAP M2 ▪ 89–113 Kent St ▪ (612) 9256 2222 ▪ www.langhamhotels. com ▪ $$$
This grand hotel oozes elegance with its marble foyer and custom-made contemporary furnishings. Rooms offer views of the western harbour or Sydney skyline.

Park Hyatt Sydney
MAP M1 ▪ 7 Hickson Rd ▪ 9256 1234 ▪ www. hyatt.com ▪ $$$
Many rooms in this luxurious six-star hotel have Opera House views, as does the rooftop heated swimming pool.

Sofitel Sydney Darling Harbour
MAP L4 ▪ 12 Darling Dr ▪ 8388 8888 ▪ www. sofitelsydneydarling harbour.com.au ▪ $$$
Contemporary rooms with floor-to-ceiling windows create an airy feel at this waterfront hotel, which has a 20-m (66-ft) infinity pool, fine French dining and harbour views from the Champagne Bar.

Crown Sydney
MAP L2 ▪ 1 Barangaroo Ave ▪ 8871 7188 ▪ www. crownsydney.com.au ▪ $$$
This six-star hotel has been curated down to the smallest details – even the air conditioning gently pumps a subtle signature fragrance throughout the building. Personalized service, great views, the finest dining and every facility imaginable: this is uncompromising luxury with a price tag to match.

The Fullerton Hotel Sydney
MAP M3 ▪ 1 Martin Place ▪ 8223 1111 ▪ www. fullertonhotels.com ▪ $$$
Set in Martin Place in the financial heart of the city, the former General Post Office building is steeped in character and elegance. It's surrounded by luxury shopping and is just a short walk away from the main harbourfront attractions, providing both comfort and convenience.

Beachside Hotels

Crowne Plaza Coogee
MAP U5 ▪ 242 Arden St ▪ 93157600 ▪ www. coogeebeach.crowne plaza.com ▪ $$
Located beside Coogee beach, the Crowne Plaza has modern rooms, most with ocean views. Relax and take a cool dip in the pool – assuming you can drag yourself away from the beach.

Hotel Ravesis
MAP H5 ▪ 118 Campbell Parade ▪ 9365 4422 ▪ www.hotelravesis. com ▪ $$
Every room of this boutique hotel in Bondi has stunning ocean views. Split-level suites cost more, but each is unique.

QT Bondi
MAP H5 ▪ 6 Beach Rd ▪ 8362 3900 ▪ www. qthotels.com ▪ $$$
A cool, surfside hotel with ocean views and a beach vibe. Rooms are spacious, with kitchenettes, and generous extras include thongs (flip flops), beach toys and snacks.

The Sebel Sydney Manly Beach
MAP U3 ▪ 8/13 S Steyne ▪ 9977 8866 ▪ www.the sebelmanlybeach.com.au ▪ $$$
Choose an ocean view room or suite with a balcony at this property on Manly's waterfront. The Sebel is a short walk from the Cabbage Tree Bay Aquatic Reserve, one of the city's best snorkelling areas.

Watsons Bay Boutique Hotel

MAP H1 ▪ 1 Military Rd ▪ 9337 5444 ▪ www.watsonsbayhotel.com.au ▪ $$$

With 32 generous suites on the shore of Sydney Harbour, staying here feels like being on a seaside holiday with a Sydney city skyline view.

Adina Apartment Hotel Bondi Beach

MAP H5 ▪ 69/73 Hall St ▪ 9300 4800 ▪ www.tfehotels.com ▪ $$

A short walk to the famous Bondi Beach, this hotel's modern and spacious studio, one- and two-bedroom apartments are surrounded by trendy restaurants, boutiques and bars. If you tire of the beach, there is an outdoor pool and fitness centre.

Boutique Hotels

Hotel Palisade

MAP L1 ▪ 35 Bettington St ▪ 9018 0123 ▪ www.hotelpalisade.com.au ▪ $$

The eight rooms in this beautifully restored boutique property are filled with eclectic furnishings and natural light, and come with harbour or city views. Deluxe rooms also feature a kitchenette and sitting area.

Spicers Potts Point

MAP P4 ▪ 122 Victoria St ▪ 1300 525 442 ▪ www.spicersretreats.com ▪ $$$

This luxurious property in leafy Victoria Street offers a home away from home with outstanding attention to detail and glamorous communal spaces. There are 20 contemporary suites and spacious rooms.

Little National Hotel Sydney

MAP M3 ▪ 26 Clarence St ▪ 9135 0222 ▪ littlenationalhotel.com.au ▪ $$

Fantastic value for a central location, with 230 small rooms and a rooftop balcony with a bar and lounge area.

The Tank Stream Hotel

MAP M3 ▪ 97–99 Pitt St ▪ 8222 1200 ▪ www.stgileshotels.com ▪ $$

Built above the freshwater stream that sustained the early European colonists, this hotel's distinctive architecture captures the wavelike form of the stream and the harbour it flows into. With contemporary finishes and a central location, it makes a great base for exploring the city.

View Sydney

MAP D1 ▪ 17 Blue St ▪ 9955 0499 ▪ www.viewhotels.com ▪ $$

Clean, comfortable and affordable rooms in a terrific location on Sydney's north side, with views across the harbour and lots of transport options on the doorstep. Upper floor rooms have the best view and less noise from the nearby train line.

Larmont Sydney by Lancemore

MAP P4 ▪ 2/14 Kings Cross Rd ▪ 9295 8888 ▪ www.lancemore.com.au ▪ $$

Stylish accommodation within walking distance of the city centre and some of Sydney's best shopping strips, cafés, bars and restaurants.

Crystalbook Albion

MAP N6 ▪ 21 Little Albion St ▪ 8029 7900 ▪ www.crystalbrookcollection.com ▪ $$

Discretely tucked down a lane in an artistic neighbourhood, this intimate, unpretentious hotel offers simple, elegant rooms, including an affordable cosy room for two that is small on space but big on style and value.

Historic Hotels

Paramount House Hotel

MAP N5 ▪ 80 Commonwealth St ▪ 9211 1222 ▪ www.paramounthousehotel.com ▪ $$

Once the headquarters of Paramount Pictures Australia, this converted Art Deco warehouse has 29 individually styled bedrooms with Italian terrazzo bathrooms and well-stocked minibars.

The Old Clare Hotel

MAP L6 ▪ 1 Kensington St ▪ 8277 8277 ▪ www.theoldclarehotel.com.au ▪ $$$

The industrial chic of the Old Clare will appeal to design lovers. Formerly home to Carlton United Breweries, the space now presents 62 rooms with one-off vintage chairs, handcrafted lighting and exposed brickwork.

Kimpton Margot Sydney

MAP M5 ▪ 339 Pitt St ▪ 8027 8000 ▪ www.ihg.com ▪ $$$

A renovated 1930s office building has been reborn as a stylish Art Deco hotel with rooftop bar and swimming pool. Spacious rooms feature vast beds.

Ovolo Woolloomooloo
MAP P3 ■ 6 Cowper Wharf Roadway ■ 9331 9000 ■ www.ovolo hotels.com ■ $$$

Set in a peaceful location on a historic wharf with some of Sydney's best restaurants as neighbours. A lovely melding of heritage and modern luxury, the Woolloomooloo offers a blend of rich history and sophisticated modern design.

Veriu Broadway
MAP K6 ■ 35 Mountain St ■ 8279 7880 ■ www.veriu.com.au ■ $$

On the edge of the city, this converted Federation-era warehouse and leather tannery provides comfortably affordable accomodation. It's a short stroll to cafés, shopping and public transport, with complimentary bicycles for those who prefer to ride to the city.

The Woolstore 1888 by Ovolo
MAP L4 ■ 139 Murray St ■ 8586 1888 ■ www.ovolohotels.com ■ $$

A chic conversion of a heritage building steeped in the area's industrial and working-class history. The former wool store combines the comfort, style and sophistication of contemporary design with industrial-chic interiors and art-splashed walls, with vibrant inner-city culture on the doorstep.

The Grace Sydney
MAP M3 ■ 77 York St ■ 9272 6888 ■ www.gracehotel.com.au ■ $$

There is elegance at every turn in this beautifully restored 387-room hotel in the city centre. The former 1920s department store effortlessly blends Neo-Gothic architecture with Art Deco interiors and old-fashioned charm, finished with plenty of modern comforts.

Serviced Apartments

Adina Surry Hills
MAP D5 ■ 359 Crown St ■ 8302 1000 ■ www.adinahotels.com ■ $$

Close to the Crown Street bars and restaurants, Sydney Cricket Ground and the Entertainment Quarter, this hotel is also right above the legendary Bills restaurant.

Bondi 38
MAP H5 ■ 38 Campbell Parade ■ 409 946 313 ■ www.bondi38.com.au ■ $$$

These studios and one- or two-bedroom apartments are a home from home. Directly across the road from the beach, they have outstanding views and are just far enough off the centre of the strip for relative peace and quiet.

Fraser Suites
MAP M4 ■ 488 Kent St ■ 8823 8888 ■ www.frasershospitality.com ■ $$

More than 200 studio and one-bedroom apartments with well-equipped kitchenettes located right by Town Hall Station. The building features a fully equipped gym and pool.

Meriton Suites World Tower
MAP M5 ■ 95 Liverpool Street ■ 8263 7500 ■ www.meritonsuites.com.au ■ $$$

Get a bird's-eye view of the city in one of the 115 rooms in Sydney's tallest building, with outstanding views out to sea.

Skye Suites Sydney
MAP M3 ■ 300 Kent St ■ 9052 7588 ■ www.skyesuites.com.au ■ $$

This tall building has 73 spacious studio, one- and two-bedroom open-plan apartments, designed by award-winning architect Koichi Takada. The pool and gym alone are good reasons to stay here.

Quest Manly
MAP U3 ■ 54–68 West Esplanade ■ 9976 4600 ■ www.questapartments.com.au ■ $$

Step off the ferry from the city and into this lovely accommodation offering 53 studio, one- and two-bedroom apartments with harbour views. It's within easy walking distance of the beach, as well as all the cafés, restaurants and other attractions relaxed Manly has to offer.

Budget Hotels

Hotel Challis
MAP P3 ■ 21–23 Challis Ave ■ 9192 9000 ■ www.hotelchallispottspoint.com ■ $

Located on one of Potts Point's prettiest streets, this Victorian terrace comprises 51 rooms, some with balconies.

The Maisonette Potts Point
MAP P3 ■ 31 Challis Ave ■ 9357 3878 ■ www.themaisonette.com.au ■ $

This guesthouse offers single and double rooms with shared bathrooms, and is perfect for those wanting a little more privacy than a hostel.

Sydney Harbour YHA

MAP M2 ▪ 110 Cumberland St ▪ 8272 0900 ▪ www.yha.com.au ▪ $
This is the only backpacker hostel in the Rocks, and has great views from the roof terrace.

Wake Up Bondi

MAP H5 ▪ 110 Campbell Parade ▪ 9130 4660 ▪ www.wakeup.com.au ▪ $
Directly opposite Bondi Beach, this relaxed hostel runs a good selection of daily activities.

Wake Up Sydney

MAP M6 ▪ 509 Pitt St ▪ 9288 7888 ▪ www.wakeup.com.au ▪ $
This award-winning, 500-bed hostel offers sparkling-clean facilities with a friendly on-site bar and restaurant.

Sydney Park Hotel

MAP B6 ▪ 631 King St ▪ 9557 1188 ▪ www.sydneyparkhotel.com.au ▪ $
This heritage-listed pub near the airport has eight rooms with vintage and custom-made furniture. An inner-city train station lies across the road, and Newtown's trendy shops, cafés and restaurants are on the doorstep.

The Urban Newtown

MAP B6 ▪ 52–60 Enmore Rd ▪ 8960 7800 ▪ www.theurbannewtown.com.au ▪ $
Close to the city in the middle of funky Newtown, this is a convenient spot for diverse nightlife – it's within walking distance of entertainment venues and eateries along vibrant King Street and Enmore Road. The stylish studio rooms have an appealing industrial design.

Terminus Hotel Pyrmont

MAP K3 ▪ 61 Harris St ▪ 9692 0301 ▪ www.terminuspyrmont.com ▪ $
A historic pub with nine stylishly appointed double rooms (two with private ensuite) in the heart of habourside Pyrmont – a working-class industrial suburb turned gentrified city playground. Nearby are plenty of wonderful breakfast cafés and evening bars, as well as the many attractions of Darling Harbour.

Beyond Sydney

Lilianfels

5/19 Lilianfels Ave, Katoomba ▪ 4780 1200 ▪ www.lilianfels.com.au ▪ $$$
This haven, where civilization meets with wilderness, is tucked away at the end of the main street in the Blue Mountains town of Katoomba. Sweeping views of the Jamison Valley can be enjoyed from the charming rooms, and there is genteel fine dining at the on-site restaurant.

The Carrington Hotel

15–47 Katoomba St, Katoomba ▪ 4782 1111 ▪ www.thecarrington.com.au ▪ $$
A beautiful property steeped in the history and elegance of a bygone era, this was the preferred Blue Mountains retreat of Sydney's elite in the 1900s. Centrally located in Katoomba's main street, it is surrounded by galleries, cafés and the expansive Blue Mountains National Park.

Crowne Plaza Hunter Valley

▪ 430 Wine Country Dr, Lovedale ▪ 4991 0000 ▪ www.crowneplazahuntervalley.com.au ▪ $$
Located in the heart of New South Wales's iconic winemaking region, this conveniently located spot is a great base for exploring the area's vineyards and wineries. The stylish accommodation is complemented by expansive, manicured grounds, good service and on-site dining options.

Spicers Vineyards Estate

555 Hermitage Rd, Pokolbin ▪ 1300 192 868 ▪ www.spicersretreats.com ▪ $$$
A tranquil escape from the busy city, this Hunter Valley hotel has 12 luxurious guest rooms, which each come with their own fireplace and a romantic setting amid natural bushland. There is also a private vineyard and an award-winning restaurant that serves modern Australian dishes made from ingredients grown on site.

Peppers Manor House

Kater Rd, Suttons Forest ▪ 1300 092 876 ▪ www.peppers.com.au ▪ $$
This grand country house, formerly the residence of a pioneering farming family, is set on an expansive Southern Highlands estate and oozes country charm. It's a place for refined relaxation: snuggle up in front of the cosy fireplaces in winter, and enjoy poolside drinks in the shade of the leafy courtyards in summer.

General Index

Acknowledgments

This edition updated by

Contributor Deborah Soden

Senior Editor Alison McGill

Senior Designer Stuti Tiwari

Project Editor Elspeth Beidas

Project Art Editor Bharti Karakoti

Editors Avanika, Guy Croton

Designer Tessa Bindloss

Proofreader Kathryn Glendenning

Indexer Hilary Bird

Picture Researcher Sharon Southren

Picture Research Administrator Vagisha Pushp

Publishing Assistant Halima Mohammed

Jacket Designer Jordan Lambley

Senior Cartographic Editor Casper Morris, Subhashree Bharti

Cartographic Editor Ed Merritt

Cartography Manager Suresh Kumar

Senior Production Editor Jason Little

Production Controller Samantha Cross

Managing Editors Shikha Kulkarni, Hollie Teague

Deputy Editorial Manager Beverly Smart

Managing Art Editor Sarah Snelling

Senior Managing Art Editor Priyanka Thakur

Art Director Maxine Pedliham

Publishing Director Georgina Dee

The publisher would like to thank the following for their kind permission to reproduce their photographs:

(Key: a-above; b-below/bottom; c-centre; f-far; l-left; r-right; t-top)

123RF.com: boggy22 120tl, Andras Deak 4clb, dinozzaver 4cla, Aurelien Ducos 122t, iamjazz-dog 115br, jovannig 13crb, 47b, Chee-Onn Leong 86cla, Ikonya 88b, Bruce Palme 57cl, Claudia Schnepf 107t, Leah-Anne Thompson 137tl

Alamy Stock Photo: Allstar Picture Library 110 45cl, Martin Berry 10bl, 48tl, 60b, 102tl, 131crb, 139br, Paul Brown 4cr, chris24 17, Colport 44t, Zoltán Csipke 75tr, CulturalEyes - AusGS2 71tr, Richard Cummins 23br, Ian Dagnall 80bl, 93cra, Ian G Dagnall 22clb, domonabike 75cl, Stephen Dwyer 3tr, 140-41, Jackie Ellis 25bl, Julio Etchart 100c, Greg Balfour Evans 126tl, Ilya Genkin 6cla, Manfred Gottschalk 41cl, 134b, Jeffrey Isaac Greenberg 7+ 74br, Andre van Huizen 74t, Ian Dagnall Commercial Collection 28cra, Jeffrey Isaac Greenberg 20+ 46clb, Graham Jepson 46tr, 121t, Bjanka Kadic

48b, 51tr, Paul Lovelace 37bl, 95t, 119br, mauritius images GmbH / Matthias Tunger 52tr, MB_Photo 4b, Richard Milnes 52bl, 53tr, 53clb, mjmediabox 12bl, 72tl, 73b, Martin Norris 102-03b, Samantha Ohlsen 18cra, 61br, Ozimages 138cb, picturelibrary 30-31b, Robertharding / Marco Simoni 22-23c, RooM the Agency / janetteasche 108-09b, Will Steeley 101br, Stonemeadow Photography 64-65b, Vidimages 33b, Wallace Media Network / Robert Wallace 62cl, Robert Wallwork 21b, Michael Willis 60tr, Wongalea 107br

American Express Openair Cinemas: 83tr

Andrew McDonald Shoemaker: 91cb

Art Gallery Of New South Wales: Jenni Carter 31tr, Felicity Jenkins 11tl

Australian Chamber Orchestra: Wolter Peeters 69cl

Australian National Maritime Museum: James Horan Photography 67tr

Australian Reptile Park: 138tl

Barangaroo: 11crb, 36bl, 37tl

Bodhi Restaurant: 4cl, 99c

Elise Brennan: 104tl, 114tl, 117tl, 118tl

BridgeClimb Sydney: 16br

Carriageworks: Jacquie Manning 116b

Centennial Parklands: 66br

Chat Thai: 92c

City Recital Hall: Nick Gilbert 73tl

Commune: 110t

Contessa Balmain: 125br

Dear Sainte Eloise: Nikki To 98t

Dreamstime.com: Leonid Andronov 36-37ca, Rafael Ben Ari 23tl, Beataaldridge 76bl, Gordon Bell 20tl, Bennymarty 10cl, Riccardo Biondani 12-13ca, Dan Breckwoldt 56-57b, Richie Chan 30cra, 89cla, Elizabeth Coughlan 11ca, David Dennis 19c, Davide Lo Dico 10crb, Donnabremer 65tr, Esmehelit 26-27, Filedimage 38-39c, 127tr, Giovanni Gagliardi 3tl, 84-85, Markus Gann 101tl, Julian Gazzard 136bl, Eric Isselâe / Isselee 39br, Jackmalipan 11bl, Gerd Kohlmus 130t, Ingus Kruklitis 10clb, Robyn Mackenzie 76tr, Magspace 58tl, 123bl, Martingraf 25tr, Bundit Minramun 34br, 51clb, 81tr, 115tl, Mkojot 90bl, Nyker1 16cla, Sathit Plengchawee 106tl, Pominoz 63bl, 87br, Lester Riley 129bl, Constantin Stanciu 38bl, Lim Yong Tick 17tl, Gordon Tipene 2tl, 8-9, Tktktk 91tr, Aleksandar Todorovic 24bl, Julien Viry 7br, 35tr, 97bl, Vselenka 83cl, Taras Vyshnya 59b, Juergen Wallstabe 112-13, Bruce Whittingham 19tl, 57tr, 58bl, Zeytun Images 96tr, 96bl

Empire Lounge: 111ca

The Fenwick: 125c

Gallon Pyrmont: 124tr

Getty Images: AFP / Greg Wood 82br, AFP / Peter Parks 82tl, Corbis Historical / Hulton Deutsch 15b, Fairfax Media / Frank Burke 14cr, Fairfax Media / The AGE / Sebastian Costanzo 63tr, Fairfax Media / The Sydney Morning Herald / Andrew Taylor 45tr, Fairfax Media Archives / Craig Golding 32cra, Fairfax Media Archives / Frank Albert Charles Burke 14bl, Chris Hyde 33tl, Andreas Rentz 21cr, Patrick Riviere 32bl, Wayne Taylor 77tr, wallix 24-25c, Lisa Maree Williams 15tl, 54tl, WireImage / Don Arnold 68t, 69tr

Getty Images / iStock: benedek 128t, Camila1111 40-41b, ChristianB 133tl, DarrenTierney 2tr, 42-43, DuncanSharrocks 12cla, E+ / davidf 21tl, E+ / Drazen_ 40cla, E+ / mikulas1 133br, E+ / Veni 135tl, jamenpercy 4t, KHellon 10ca, kitz-travellers 94tl, kokkai 4crb, LenSoMy 87t, NCHANT 29b, RugliG 62tr, t_rust 29tl, zetter 34-35t

I'm Free Walking Tours: 80tr

The Imperial Hotel: 70tr

Indigo: 111br

Kate Owen Gallery: Helen McCarthy Tyalmuty 'Untitled' 243 x 189cm, Acrylic on Linen 50br

Mamak: Alana Dimou 92br

Mary Evans Picture Library: Photo Researchers 44cb

Nutcote: Jacquie Manning 54b

Opera Australia: Prudence Upton 68br

The Oxford Hotel: 71bl

Shutterstock.com: frenchiestravel 78-79, Nils Jorgensen 55tr, marcobrivio.photo 56ca, MOLPIX 132tl, OKMG 77clb, Richard Sowersby 41ca, Tooykrub 121br, Taras Vyshnya 1, 18-19b

Spice I Am: 105br

State Library of New South Wales: 66t

Sydney Jewish Museum: 49tl

Sydney Living Museums: Susannah Place Museum / James Horan 22br

Taronga Conservation Society Australia: 39tl

The Bookshop Darlinghurst: 70clb

White Rabbit Gallery: Yang Wei-Lin 50t

Writing NSW: Boundless Festival 55cl

Cover images:

Front and Spine: **Shutterstock.com:** Taras Vyshnya; *Back:* **Dreamstime.com:** Jackmalipan crb, Mdworschak tr; **Getty Images:** Stone / Manfred Gottschalk cla; **Shutterstock.com:** Rudy Balasko tl, Taras Vyshnya b

Pull-out Map Cover:

Shutterstock.com: Taras Vyshnya

All other images © Dorling Kindersley

Penguin
Random
House

First edition 2005

Published in Great Britain by
Dorling Kindersley Limited
DK, One Embassy Gardens, 8 Viaduct
Gardens, London SW11 7BW, UK

The authorised representative in the EEA is
Dorling Kindersley Verlag GmbH. Arnulfstr.
124, 80636 Munich, Germany

Published in the United States by
DK Publishing, 1745 Broadway, 20th Floor,
New York, NY 10019, USA

Copyright © 2005, 2022 Dorling
Kindersley Limited
A Penguin Random House Company

22 23 24 25 10 9 8 7 6 5 4 3 2 1

A CIP catalogue record is available
from the British Library.

A catalogue record for this book is available
from the Library of Congress.

ISSN 1479-344X
ISBN 978 0 2414 1848 2

Printed and bound in China

www.dk.com

As a guide to abbreviations in visitor information blocks: **Adm** = admission charge; **D** = dinner; **L** = lunch.

Selected Street Index